Stephen Covey: "Communication is the most important skill in life"

Sir Richard Branson: "Communication is the most important skill any leader can possess"

COMMUNICATING YOUR PERSONAL BRAND

Lessons from India and the west on how to win jobs and lead people by jumping out of the box of personal limitation

STEPHEN MANALLACK

To find out more about this book or
to contact the author, please visit:
www.vividpublishing.com.au/communicatingyourpersonalbrand

Copyright © 2016 Stephen Manallack

ISBN: 978-1-925442-23-6

Published by Vivid Publishing
P.O. Box 948, Fremantle Western Australia 6959
www.vividpublishing.com.au

Cataloguing-in-Publication data is available from the National Library of Australia

Subjects include: Personal brand, leadership skills, persuasion and presentations,
speaking and communication, your image.

CHAPTERS

ABOUT THE AUTHOR

Stephen Manallack is a Public Relations consultant and Author who has spent the last decade working across borders – east and west. He is a Director of India and Asia business consultancy EastWest Academy and the author of three books including *Soft Skills for a Flat World* published by Tata McGraw-Hill India – providing insights into the "10 mindsets" of Indian business. He writes an occasional blog for Australia India Institute. He serves on the Judging Panel for the Annual Business Awards of the Indian Executive Club in Melbourne. Stephen's first book, *You Can Communicate*, was published by Pearson Education in 2002. His second, *Riding the Elephant – Doing Business and Making Profits in Modern India* Melbourne Books in 2010.

With his work and teaching in mind training and meditation, Stephen has learned how to combine mindset – drawing ideas from east and west – and soft skills to become a more effective communicator and leader. His commitment is to leadership based on strong values such as honesty, generosity and patience – to communication based on truth, friendship and inspiring others.

Other books by Stephen Manallack

Soft Skills for a Flat World
Tata McGraw-Hill India
2012

Riding the Elephant – Investing and Doing Business in Modern India
Melbourne Books
2010

You Can Communicate
Pearson Education
2002

JUMP OUT OF THE BOX

Too many of us are living as if stuck in a box – a self-imposed box that feels safe and secure but which actually limits our success and happiness, making us miserable, unable to face change, blind to real opportunity, surrounded by people who are also content to live in boxes.

Sometimes we open the lid and peek out of the box, and occasionally we leave it and walk outside – but mostly we return to this artificial feeling of safety and security. "Artificial" feeling, because the box is neither safe nor secure – every moment we sit isolated in this box, the world outside is changing. This means every time we peek out or walk out, the world seems more and more confronting and confusing, and we climb back in.

Worse still, in the box life itself seems to be flying by, time goes fast, the world is just in too much of a hurry and we wonder what it could all be about. In this way, we cannot see our purpose, we take no steps towards it and the opportunity is gone.

Opening up to real communication – revealing and sharing the real you – is the biggest step you can take to be free of the box.

This book provides a way – better communication of your personal brand – to jump out of that box of self-imposed limitation and find your life purpose, true happiness and success.

Life is all about relationships. To be happy and fulfilled, each one of us desperately wants strong relationships, where stories are shared, where love and listening go together and where communication is a genuine sharing. With values such as generosity, ethics and patience, you cannot go wrong. So – tell your story, listen and connect with others. Talk, listen and connect.

WHY THIS BOOK IS A MUST READ FOR YOUR FUTURE SUCCESS

"Communication is the most important skill in life"

Would you like your leadership brand to be based on strong values such as generosity, ethics and patience? Could you be a leader who disrupts and innovates? Can your personal communication be based on truth, friendship and inspiring others?

By changing the way you see yourself, and changing the way others see you, your real leadership brand can develop and inspire others.

What is holding back your success? Chances are you are sitting in a small box – the box of limitations, of fears, anxiety, isolation and lack of real connection. The only way to break out of this box is through communication of your brand – revealing and sharing the real you.

The experts tell us that things like happiness, pleasure and success are contagious – when we choose to spend time with happy people, we take on happiness too. But they also tell us that misery loves company – that is, when we are miserable we seek out others who are miserable too. Spending more time with happy and successful people contributes to our own happiness and success. Misery finds more misery – which is like retreating into a small box where we are closed off from everything except other people who are miserable too.

This is the box of self-imposed limitations, fearful of connection, wary of others, cynical about the world and separating us from happiness and success.

How you see yourself right now could be like sitting in that small box – success and happiness will only come if you change the way you see yourself and jump out of the box. But it takes courage to become the leader who jumped out of the box – courage because you will have to make many changes. It takes courage, because you will reveal your personal brand like never before.

The first big change is to accept that in a modern world it is not enough to be very good at what you do – whether your skill is a profession, science, IT, engineering, health, a trade, finance or consulting. In addition to being the best at what you do, you have to have an impact on those you serve – a personal brand – and this comes down to improving your communication and leadership.

If all you focus on is being the best at what you do, you will place yourself in a small box and not reach the leadership potential that is within you. Why? Because when you are in the box others cannot even see your potential. The way to break out of this box is by adding powerful communication to your existing skills.

When Stephen Covey, author of 7 HABITS OF HIGHLY EFFECTIVE PEOPLE, wrote that "Communication is the most important skill in life" the world had not yet become fully connected and linked. Now we live in the flat world where we are all connected and what happens in one part of the world is also having impact everywhere else. So this book extends the Covey quote – "GLOBAL communication is the most important skill in life". Whatever your career, whatever you do in your working life, to succeed you will need to communicate well with people from all around this world – this book makes you ready for that success.

In this book you will learn how to:

- Communicate your personal brand
- Gain global communication skills
- Build cross cultural communication skills
- Build presentation and public speaking skills
- Create teamwork across borders

Which means you will be ready to gain that promotion or provide the leadership which leads to success.

Is this book right for you?

If you are a University and IIT student or currently a post graduate student, this book prepares you for the next phase – getting that great job. Are you a new employee? This book will teach you how to relate to those above you, and other new hires as well. You will become a better team player and contributor, which means your career is on an upward trend.

You might be a young professional and young executive, facing real communication challenges already. Meet those challenges, get your message across and become vastly more effective at what you do now – by building your personal brand. You could be in management – either junior manager or even someone who has been in management for some time and wants to get better. You are bound to be of entrepreneurial mindset and a future leader, and you know that success depends on your ability to convince and lead others, to persuade and create new markets and new products. Communication is the biggest step you can take towards a positive personal brand – which leads to a better career and successful life.

Do you really know what employers want? What they want will determine how successful you are at gaining employment and winning promotion. This was summed up in the Financial Times "What do employers want? In two words: soft skills."

Kumar Mangalam Birla is the Chairman of The Aditya Birla Group and a man of significant standing in India. He highlights the important of being a global manager – "Our efforts in this area have been directed at building not an 'Indian manager who works internationally' but a 'global manager who happens to be Indian'."

Do you know what Mr Birla says about leadership? As a future leader, you should know –

"Leadership is all about plugging in to the minds and hearts of people. It is about rallying them around to a compelling and exciting vision of the future. It is about upping the imagination of the organisation. It is about encouraging a spirit of intellectual ferment and constructive dissent so that people are not bound by the status quo, and mavericks are given space and free play."

And Sir Richard Branson put it right there – "Communication is the most important skill any leader can possess."

Our focus is on global communication skills based on values and the mind of success. Rabindranath Tagore gives you a call to action: "You can't cross the sea merely by standing and staring at the water." Start now on the path to creating your personal brand via better global communication skills – the path to promotion and leading people.

Find your leadership – change the way you see yourself and the way others see you. Build relationships through positive communication. Jump out of that small box of limitation and become the leader you can be – the leader who jumped out of the box.

THRIVING BY ADAPTING TO CHANGE

The soft skill everybody overlooks and you won't get in any other communication book is the capacity to thrive and adapt to change.

From my association with India and some of the great modern business leaders there, I began a journey to realise that the biggest soft skill of all is the ability to live successfully with change – constant, unpredictable change. No other soft skills book or course shows you how to do this, yet it is central to communication success.

Promotion – the thing you want – is itself a big change and those making decisions about your future will be contemplating just how well you adapt to change. Leading people is a constantly changing task, meaning you have to be flexible and adaptable – you need to thrive in change.

People who fear change are the ones who stay stuck in the small box of limited potential. People who break out of the box and go on to lead are the ones who embrace change.

By changing the way you see yourself, and changing the way others see you, your personal brand and real leadership can develop and inspire others.

The first big change is to accept that in a modern world it is not enough to be very good at what you do – whether your skill is a profession, science, IT, engineering, health, a trade, finance or consulting. In addition to being the best at what you do, you have to have an impact on those you serve and this comes down to improving your communication and leadership. In that way, you create a positive personal brand.

You can improve communication by studying how business communicates, but also making big advances if we combine this with the wisdom of the ages, with the thoughts of great thinkers and spiritual leaders.

For example, in the chapter in *You Can Communicate* on "Making New Friends" I explained that one of the barriers is that we make assumptions about people that often turn out wrong. If we assume a person is not interested in us, we become tongue tied or stay away – it is the assumption that is the barrier. There is an alternative and I could find no better source than this quote from His Holiness the Dalai Lama: "Wherever I meet people, I always have the feeling that I am encountering another human being, just like myself. I find it is much easier to communicate with others on that level. If we emphasise specific characteristics, like I am Tibetan or I am Buddhist, then there are differences. But those things are secondary. If we can leave the differences aside, I think we can easily communicate, exchange ideas and share experiences." This is a great soft skills lesson.

This western and eastern thought process was so beautifully developed by a western nun and great author in the Tibetan Buddhist tradition, Pema Chodron, who said: "When you open yourself to the continually changing, impermanent, dynamic nature of your own being and of reality, you increase your capacity to love and care about other people and your capacity to not be afraid. You're able to keep your eyes open, your heart open, and your mind open. And you notice when you get caught up in prejudice, bias, and aggression. You develop an enthusiasm for no longer watering those negative seeds, from now until the day you die. And, you begin to think of your life as offering endless opportunities to start to do things differently."

But this attitude needs to be combined with some of the communication lessons from corporate communication, showing how we can be more successful making new friends and lead by:

- Listening to people
- Speaking in ways they understand
- Not being scared of being different
- Creating something interesting to do
- Making relationships fun

Effective business leaders have the art of using the right words at the right time; this time I like a combination of my grandmother and the Buddha for inspiration. Grandma used to put it this way: "If you can't say something nice, say nothing." This is a wise caution against being too critical of others. She would have liked this quote from the Buddha: "If you know anything that's hurtful and untrue, don't say it. If you know anything that's helpful and untrue, don't say it. If you know anything that is hurtful and true, don't say it. If you know anything that is helpful and true, find the right time."

I have seen "finding the right time" work well for good Indian corporate leaders. If you find the right time to say something, it generally works. If you say it at the wrong time, it can lead to confusion or hostility. The best way to improve your timing is to improve your listening. That way, you know what is on the mind of the other person. You can then pick the moment. Whether it is coincidence or whatever, there is always opportunity, as Deepak Chopra, an Indian-born USA-based writer and speaker on self-help and spirituality, has said: "When you live your life with an appreciation of coincidences and their meanings, you connect with the underlying field of infinite possibilities."

However, even the best leaders and communicators sometimes face change and obstacles – Deepak Chopra again: "Even when you think you have your life all mapped out, things happen that shape your destiny in ways you might never have imagined."

I've spoken at many corporate communication sessions, and here is my adaptation of some of the best messages to help you control stress and minimise selfish outbursts:

- Take breaks, stand up, breathe deeply, be alone, slow your thoughts

- Make life simpler (too much stress comes from trivia)
- Use delays positively – when caught in traffic, breathe deeply
- Do something each day that you really like to do
- Force yourself to talk over difficult things – once you start, it becomes easier
- Learn how to say "No" in a positive, friendly way, not closing doors
- Take a walk, use the stairs, go out and relax
- Do unpleasant tasks now – it takes less energy than worrying all day

Notice how much of our time is spent talking about what other people *should* do? This thinking is a waste of time – few successful Indian business leaders focus much of their attention on what should be, because they are so focused on what is and what it might become. It is surprising how many people do not know that the best way to improve any relationship is to forget yourself and focus on the other person. Change yourself – don't wait for them to change. Taken further, good listening skills seem to be in decline. And few people know that in order to like other people, we first need to know and like ourselves. Yet we're all too busy coping with daily life to stop and reflect: "Who am I?' or even "What do I want?"

Again, for inspiration turn to the writings of His Holiness the Dalai Lama: "If you want to change the world, first try to improve and bring about change within yourself. That will help change your family. From there it just gets bigger and bigger. Everything we do has some effect, some impact." Sir Richard Branson extends this theme into looking for the positive rather than the negative: "…it is necessary to give other people the space to thrive, to catch people doing something right, rather than getting things wrong."

A leader who knows, even enjoys, impermanence, is Kiran Mazumdar-Shaw, the Chairperson and Managing Director of Biocon Ltd and one of India's most successful and wealthiest women. She is like a beacon of hope. Her company, Biocon Ltd, is a global player in pharmaceuticals and biotechnology. Yet many times her chosen path came to a brick wall – she faced occasions of rejection. She achieved success because of her ability to adapt to change – "I certainly believe that everything happens with a reason. I wanted to join medical school and when that did not happen I took up biology instead. And that led me to specialise in brewing. However when I was not accepted as a brew master in India, I turned to biotechnology in a very accidental manner. In hindsight, I am grateful that the brewing doors shut on me and I set up Biocon instead!" She is a role model for dealing with adversity and also adapting to change.

There are occasions when we cannot do anything about the changes we experience – the best response to this was so well expressed by the great Dr A.P.J. Abdul Kalam, former President of India (2002-07): "I was willing to accept what I couldn't change".

This process of change, personal and impersonal, internal and external goes on constantly even without us noticing it, and it affects us intimately in our daily life. This impermanence should not be something we fear – rather, it encourages us to follow our heart and get on with reaching our potential. Steve Jobs, Founder of Apple, told a Stanford University group: "Your time is limited, so don't waste it living someone else's life. Don't be trapped by dogma, which is living with the results of other people's thinking. Don't let the noise of other's opinions drown out your inner voice. Most important, have the courage to follow your heart and intuition. They somehow already know what you truly want to become. Everything else is secondary."

Finally, impermanence is an aid to the understanding of the ultimate nature of things. Seeing that all things are perishable, and change at any moment, we also begin to see that things have no great substantial existence or attraction of their own. Seeing this, we head towards freedom. John F. Kennedy was President of the USA for such a short time, but left a legacy of great ideas and insightful quotes. Consider this: "Change is the law of life. And those who look only to the past or present are certain to miss the future." With this inspiration, make sure you do not miss the great future.

Tibet's Dalai Lama extends this point: "From early morning until late into the night, even in our dreams, we experience all kinds of perceptions. We go from being relaxed to being anxious, we sometimes feel anger, sometimes desire, other times joy and compassion. We can be sad, then happy. These are transitory states of mind – they are impermanent, they come and go, from moment to moment. But there must be something deeper that is aware of all this – our true Buddha nature – but this is usually hidden by us as we cling to momentary feelings. So we remove the clinging, like opening a curtain, and see our true self. Open, spacious, calm, aware…"

Sir Richard Branson put it right there – "Communication is the most important skill any leader can possess." Find your leadership through better communication – break out of that small box – change the way you see yourself and the way others see you.

THE ART OF CONVERSATION AND YOUR BRAND

Conversation creates understanding. With understanding, you become a real leader. That is why the art of conversation should be part of your personal brand. Your leadership can be based on strong values such as honesty, generosity and patience, and this needs to shine in how you deal with others. Your personal communication and conversation skills lead others if based on truth, friendship and inspiring others to reach their potential.

In conversation as in other parts of communication, by changing the way you see yourself, and changing the way others see you, your real leadership can develop and inspire others. That becomes a personal brand that attracts others, leading to success and achievement.

People who stay in that small box of restriction and limitation don't seem to talk a lot – they miss out on friendship and social connection, they never become leaders. It takes courage to become a conversationalist, to reach out to others and take the risk of connecting – that is, to jump out of the box.

There is a powerful business benefit in learning how to create trust and enthusiasm within workplaces through the Art of Conversation. Most good conversations are based on stories, and this applies to business as much as to the personal front. With genuine conversation, not only is the work experience improved, but decisions and the agreed directions become clearer because conversation creates understanding. Lofty instructions do not do it, nor do those exhausting and lengthy quizzing sessions that pass for meetings in many offices.

There are six ways to create success through the Art of Conversation.

1. Be a good host

- If colleagues are early, be sure they feel welcome and comfortable. This includes offering them refreshment and reading material. You might briefly say hello, even if you can't meet with them just yet.

- Have a plan for the meeting, and share this with them.
- Monitor the time – keep it moving in a businesslike and friendly way. If meetings often go overtime, allocate more time. Don't think the length of the meeting is a measure of quality.
- Allow for short breaks if needed, a few moments of stretching the legs can make the second half as active as the first.
- Reduce interruptions because you have nothing better to do right now than meet with them, giving them your complete attention.
- If you genuinely "like" people and look forward to catching up, this attitude will show through in your eyes and your body language.

2. Extract information in a friendly way

- If you ask too many questions or produce too many forms, people will suffer fatigue and their recollections become confused. Short term you might get a result, but long term problems are on the way.

- When you need staff to spend some time giving information, be sympathetic and explain the importance of it.
- Try to extract information in the flow of the conversation, rather than having a set list of questions. This makes it less of an interrogation and more a shared experience.

3. Listen

- The words "listen" and "silent" have the same letters, for much the same reason that we have two ears and one mouth.
- Only through listening can you judge a level of understanding and potential for confusion and worry. That way you can plant the seeds of confidence instead of fuelling the fires of fear.
- We listen to people we like and talk over people we think are not as smart as us. How do you rate?

4. Become a story-teller

- The best leaders gain followers by telling stories, not by listing features, promoting benefits or issuing orders. We love to hear stories. Think about the conference speaker you really liked; chances are they were telling you stories about their life.

- Making complexity simple is a way of thinking and a challenge for everyone.
- Avoid becoming an habitual "qualifier", the kind who makes a nice simple statement about a direction and instead of waiting to hear a response launches into difficulties and side issues.
- Make sure that your firm has its stories do, for these define your brand.

5. Give people space

- Giving space is like giving respect and like showing that you care. Remember, nobody cares how much you know until they know how much you care.
- Leave space for people to put your course of action into their own words. Encourage this, and they will often bring it to a conclusion.

6. Evaluate and improve

- Create a "conversational" office culture.
- After each meeting, make a few notes on what you did well, where you missed and

how to improve. This makes you mindful of communication, and that makes you better at the art of conversation.

Conversation is not just "chatter" – it is one of the biggest ways you can change the way others see you, and through that change you jump out of the box and become the leader you know you can be.

LESSONS FROM PR FOR PERSONAL AND BUSINESS SUCCESS

You might be a young professional and young executive, your qualifications are good and your work is of a high level – but others are gaining promotion before you. You could be in management – either junior manager or even someone who has been in management for some time and you make a big contribution – but you win little praise and are overlooked when it matters. You could be of entrepreneurial mindset and a future leader, but things seem to be standing still.

What is happening here to stall your career and hold back success? Chances are you are sitting in a small box – the box of limitations, of fears, anxiety, isolation and lack of real connection.

If we were to ask what is your personal brand you probably would not have an answer. If you do not know what your brand is, how can you expect others to see it and to be aware of your potential? The only way to break out of this box is through communication – revealing and sharing the real you.

Success depends on your ability to convince and lead others, to persuade and create new markets and new products. You might be uncertain about your ability to convince others – well, you need to change the way you think about yourself, and only then will others change the way they think about you. If you recognise your inner leader and develop your personal brand, others will see your real leadership potential.

Communication is the biggest step you can take towards a better career and successful life.

Meet those challenges, get your message across and become vastly more effective at what you do now. Jump out of that box.

Do you really know what employers want? What they want will determine how successful you are at gaining employment and winning promotion. This was summed up in the Financial Times "What do employers want? In two words: soft skills."

Stephen Covey spent most of his lifetime studying how the really good organisations and the highly effective leaders went about their daily work. One thing kept showing up – they all worked very hard at communication. That is why in his book "The 7 Habits of Highly Effective People" (which topped the New York Times bestseller list) Covey's main message was summed up as: **"Communication is the most important skill in life"**. He found that the very best were also the very best communicators.

But, how should you do apply these PR lessons as an individual or entrepreneur?

We can all learn a lot from Public Relations – here are some guide posts taken from my lifetime in PR to help your communication improve and make real connections:

1. **Respect who you are:** As your life changes, if people see that you are true to yourself, to your family values and to your spiritual belief, you will gain their respect and their support. In corporate PR speak, we call this knowing your brand and sticking to corporate messages. One thing you could do as an individual or small business is to prepare a set of between 6 and 10 key statements which

sum up who you are, why you are special, how you add value and where you are going – you can repeat these as often as possible.

2. **Be generous with your time:** Sitting behind the desk just won't do much for you – good entrepreneurs are always giving their time to others. Join in those activities which are good, become part of worthy groups or clubs and do not forget to phone your family, friends and other people important to your life. We call this "networking" and Warren Buffett summed it up this way: "Someone's sitting in the shade today because someone else planted a tree..." – go out and plant lots of trees!

3. **Share what you know:** Too many businesses and professionals keep wonderful information locked away in their brains. Find the right time to pass knowledge on to others – sometimes you might get ripped off, but mostly what you know is the key to your success and clients and employers cannot choose you unless they get the message.

4. **Use social media:** We can make valuable connections with people if we are careful and thoughtful about using social media such as blogs, facebook and twitter. For small

business it is cheap and mostly involves a short, sharp time commitment – perhaps once or twice a day for as few as 5 minutes. But don't overdo it, and always think carefully about what you are putting on the internet – it is there forever.

5. **Learn how to speak in public:** People who can make thoughtful speeches have credibility and impact, so it is important at the beginning to learn the art of public speaking. It also makes your small group presentations better. Remember, always be honest and direct, show respect, speak when the opportunity is right and acknowledge the right of others to hold different views.

6. **Build your networks and contacts:** There are many others out there who are trying to get to your target audience, and not all of these are competitors. Collaboration is strength. Start talking to potential allies and once you meet people keep in touch with them.

7. **Write thoughtful notes, letters and emails:** Don't forget in this age of technology that a personal note or letter is powerful. If you are living away from home, speak to your parents regularly but also send them a letter – it will be well received. Do the same with

work colleagues and business contacts. Follow up every meeting and every contact with some form of note.

8. **Volunteer your skills:** Others in the community might benefit from your free time, perhaps helping those in need. Or it might be that your workplace needs a group to volunteer to organise some extra activity – be generous, volunteer! Do it with a good heart and no expectation of a return for you.

In this competitive world, you can sit in the small box wishing things would happen – or you can get out there and enjoy the communication journey. It is also wise to be wary of success, for it too can play with your mind – as Microsoft's founder, Bill Gates, said: "Success is a lousy teacher. It seduces smart people into thinking they can't lose."

In my view, the journey to personal and business success is best started with a generosity of spirit, an open mind and a tolerance of others. Remember the saying about it all starting "with a single step"? Tagore said "Everything comes to us that belongs to us if we create the capacity to receive it". Just like a boomerang – put out good things and you will get good things back. These are the kind of personal traits that gain attention, win promotion and make you a good leader of people – it is a great personal brand to aspire to.

6 WAYS TO IMPROVE COMMUNICATION ACROSS BORDERS

To become a long term success in the modern world you will need to be able to communicate across borders – to people with different languages and cultures to your own. Winning promotion and leading people are increasingly dependent on your ability to create cross border teams and solve business problems in any country you deal with.

People stuck in the box of restriction, fear, anxiety and non-communication always have trouble dealing across borders – "they" never seem to understand, "they" are the problem according to the person in the box. But the real lack of understanding and the real problem is that you have chosen to sit in a very small box. Fear of the unknown and the different are part of that small box.

We know that employers are increasingly rewarding those who can work successfully in global teams and cross border environments. While language skills might be important – and often are critically important – at a personal level you should do a lot to become more effective in cross border communication, because this increases your career prospects.

A good start is to have a positive attitude about cultural differences. Where you encounter them, study the differences, enjoy them and become sensitive to what this means for your communication. In this way, you can remain true to your own values while adapting to global demands.

A business man who has succeeded in almost every country on the globe is Sir Richard Branson – and he put it right there – "Communication is the most important skill any leader can possess."

Here are six ways to become a better communicator across borders:

SIMPLIFY AND CLARIFY YOUR MESSAGES

The key to being understood across borders is to reduce your messages and content to the core point – remove any subtle content, any qualification, ambiguity, complexity or diversion. Most westerners struggle with this when communicating in Asia because their Asian colleagues are far too polite to let you know they are confused by your messages. And westerners can misunderstand a positive response in Asia as meaning agreement and action – whereas in many cases it might not.

My favourite technique for simplicity and clarity is to stick to the 5W's in almost every significant communication during a meeting – that is – who, what, when, where and why of the situation – and adding the how. If your comments provide the 5W's, you have the best chance of getting your message across borders.

For people educated and raised in Asia, speaking up at meetings and giving feedback can be a new experience – but why not have a go? Again, a good way to get used to this is to try to be the person who can provide the 5W's of any discussion topic – that is, you become the person who clarifies and simplifies – wonderful.

FIND THE REAL MEANING

When listening across borders it is essential to search beyond the words to find the real meaning. In India for example, a "yes or no" question is always answered yes because it is rude to use no. And when your desired dinner guest says "I will try to be there" that is as near to a no as you will ever hear. Typically Asian countries prefer a long and slow circuitous route to the core issue while the westerner will often by contrast be blunt and straight to the point. Adaption on both sides helps the situation, whereas confronting the other produces a negative outcome.

One suggestion for Asia is to remember that your western colleague wants to hear any bad news that might be ahead for the project – they want to know about problems early, but also admire you if you have taken steps or can suggest a path to fix the problem. So whereas your background might be to keep negatives away from superiors, in dealing with the west try to take a two part approach of highlighting any potential problem while suggesting a solution.

BE PATIENT AND POLITE

While western business culture admires speed and action, many Asian cultures admire traits such as patience and courtesy. By pushing for an early result, the westerner can, without intention, offend their hosts who bring an ocean of patience to the negotiating table and can outlast most. The key is to start with a patient outlook, be totally polite even when frustrated and take the time necessary to get to the point.

It is incredibly useful to think about the culture of the people you are dealing with – those from an individualistic culture will want to take decisions here and now, while someone from a collective culture wants to advance the dialogue but leave time for consultation with others.

EXPECT DIFFERENT VIEWS

Your cross border meeting has gone well and the word "plan" seems to have been accepted on all sides and the plan itself is being developed. Has real communication happened? There are many views of the word "plan" – the western view based on a culture of absolutism holds planning as sacred, important and professional, while the eastern view based on a culture of relativism and change privately sees much planning as folly or at least as certainly changeable. Indeed, even signed contracts are seen as changeable.

How can people from both sides be better communicators and leaders?

From the western "absolutist" background, try to understand relativism, adapt to it and be aware that your Asian colleagues might not be going to develop and action the plan in the way you think. In this case, be patient and gain clarity – go over things again, define everything, describe everything. Then be prepared to have to start again.

From the eastern "relativist" background, try to understand absolutism, adapt to it and be aware your western colleagues want clarity and action around planning – they are much more comfortable in predictable situations, believe in project planning and want you to adapt to it. Gain a clear understanding of their expectations. Ensure you let them know when planning has gone wrong and things are not happening as expected.

RESPECT HIERARCHIES AND COLLECTIVE

Communicating across borders is going to bring you face to face with people with differing views of hierarchy (is respect earned or given) and collective (do I make decisions or must the group be involved). While some get frustrated by these differences, I find it exciting and challenging to work within the differing views. There can be another layer of complexity on these factors of hierarchy and collective – some parts of Asia operate around really strong hierarchies and yet also have decision making by collective. This apparent paradox can confuse the westerner. It is vital for west and east to help each other understand "how we do business around here" in a way that is tolerant and positive. Do your own research – who is really in control on the other side, how many might be in the collective and who are we actually talking to right now?

PREPARE FOR EMOTION

One of the cross-border differences that can cause project failure and real disruption is in how each culture handles emotion – consider the British, famous for "keeping your cool" under the most hostile of situations, or the Italians, well known for high resolution disputes over everything. You will need to know whether the culture of the country you are dealing with admires people for keeping your cool, seeming to be relaxed even under great pressure, to never raising one's voice, to be in personal and emotional control at all times – this is known as a "neutral" culture. Or you should know if it is what we call the "affective" cultures – some are in the west such as Italy and most are in the east such as India. In these cultures, voices can rise rapidly – sudden outbreaks of emotion and argument are common. Remaining calm is a challenge but is also essential and what helps here is the realisation that the emotional person on the other side of the table will also see gaining final harmony as essential – it's wise to wait.

CONCLUSION

Communicating across borders is greatly enriched by bringing an open and inquiring mind to the table, respecting cultural differences, expecting misunderstanding and different interpretations and being patient for the long haul. And for every generalisation above, you will meet individuals who are an exception to the rule – so being prepared for anything is a good mantra.

Being quick on your feet, able to adapt while remaining true to your own culture and values is the key to success across borders – and that will be the key to your personal success and ultimately become part of your personal brand. You can only achieve this if you break out of the box and take the risk of engaging – fully – with the world.

It starts with attitude – changing the way you see yourself, and changing the way others see you, then your real cross-border leadership can develop and inspire others.

USING SOCIAL MEDIA TO BUILD YOUR BRAND

India's Prime Minister Narendra Modi is perhaps the major global communicator among all political leaders today – regularly speaking to packed stadiums and conference centres. He recently spoke in Silicon Valley in the USA and said: "I see technology as a means to empower and as a tool that bridges the distance between hope and opportunity. Social media is reducing social barriers. It connects people on the strength of human values, not identities."

Modi went on to tell a packed house: "The status that now matters is not whether you are awake or asleep, but whether you are online or offline."

The value of using social media networks was best summarised by the author Malcolm

Gladwell in his best-selling book, The Tipping Point: "You need to seed the right people, to develop a word-of-mouth army." How big that army is depends on you, but some advisers suggest as you build a career you strive for at least 20 or 30 people who will act as your ambassadors. You can only really achieve this by using social networks well.

Some of the first to use social networking were creative professionals – including musicians, writers and artists. Musicians might have made a song available on a social networking page, artists placing a painting or writers exposing their thoughts and words to a wider audience online – facebook, twitter, LinkedIn and many other social networks. The benefit is you reach a larger audience and they become more engaged than via most other methods.

Jonah Berger, Wharton Marketing Professor, has said that using social networking sites or a new media endeavor such as blogging can be especially useful for workers looking to reshape their career into a new kind of profile. "People will begin to see you in that role," Berger says. "By creating these links outside of your organization, you can change your meaning to [others]."

None of this means you give up on traditional

networking – you have to do both – so continue to give business cards, go to events, play a role and make new friends.

The advantage of social networking sites is they allow large numbers of like-minded people to forge connections, not just at lunch, but across the country or even overseas, expanding their list of contacts which can in turn boost business or lead to a new career for you.

Wharton Marketing Professor Eric Bradlow, co-director of the Wharton Interactive Media Initiative, studies self-marketing for financial services professionals and he says developing a personal "brand" can be as important for a financial advisor as for a rock musician. "In these times, people need to differentiate themselves," notes Bradlow, who became interested in this topic five years ago when he learned that training for financial services professionals almost never included any education about marketing and self-promotion.

Bradlow advises people in business and the professions to come up with three words that could define their personal brand – describing a skill set or attitude or even community involvement. Then it becomes a matter of being consistent, across all social networks that you are using. This means the same message gets out – whether you are meeting face to face over coffee or networking via Facebook.

Different types of networking – traditional or new media – bring different pluses or minuses to the development of your brand. For example, if your market is young and IT switched on, social media becomes essential. But if they are elderly you will need to use more traditional ways. In general, combining traditional and social networking is the way to go.

LinkedIn is the most popular business-oriented social network and you can use various tools to extend your profile and reach. It is important to "work' the site, join groups, report activity and join in discussions. In other words, do not just join up and expect things to come to you.

On the other hand, caution and being true to your brand is important. It is amazing how many young professionals place crazy party photos on Facebook – which will not help them with that new job hunt later on.

Some tips to help you build brand via social networking:

- Content is the key, so when you tweet, or do Facebook posts, make sure you write content that is easy to read and recognisable, so that the audience can connect to it emotionally and they feel that is adds value to their daily lives. This takes some preparation, and maybe sample with friends before posting it online.

- Social media is about using the right keywords so interested people can find your conversation on social media and in turn drive the traffic back your website. Keywords need to be developed with your target audience in mind.

- Be consistent and regular with your communication. Make sure you have a balanced tone and every message supports your preferred personal brand.

- Leverage topics that are trendy on social networking sites, by adding your considered viewpoint or take on the issue or topic.

- Remember to listen – social media is a two way channel for communication – a great medium for delivering your message but it also a medium that can be used to listen. You will be amazed how much you can learn.

- You can keep the buzz going by seeking

out and posting articles or sites that really interested you and might be helpful to the target audience. Keep these in line with your personal brand.

- Social media is full of pitfalls and dangers, so exercise common sense and, if in doubt, leave it out. Here are some pitfalls:

- People have found themselves in legal trouble when strongly criticising a major corporation or a consumer brand. Remember, they have more money than you so the legal system is more accessible to them.

- Over the top self-promotion or over-selling is a real negative and switches your target audience right off. The danger is you appear self-obsessed – so always remember to give them plenty of what they want, be helpful to others. Linking in with some current information is one safe way to build a reputation for being useful and helpful.

- If your message is not fresh, it will seem like boring repetition.

- Be careful – it is better to draft what you want to say today and leave it until tomorrow to post it online.

- It is important to put your phone or i-pad to one side during meetings – unless there is a specific need for it. If you are constantly looking at a screen while others are teaming up to solve problems or build a program, you will look as if you are not interested and you will almost certainly miss important information.
- There is a time for social media and a time for face-to-face communication. One guiding principle is that anything really important to a relationship should be said face-to-face. It might then be reinforced by social media. If, for example, you need to apologise to someone, always first do it personally before committing to any social media.

Peter S. Fader, Wharton Marketing Professor and co-director of the Wharton Interactive Media Initiative, says establishing a personal brand is important in an age in which consumers are more skeptical and seeking a level of comfort and trust. "Before, receivers would usually play a passive role and accept a product because it was there. Now, they want to know what your source of credibility is and why they should trust you."

But building an online identity takes patience – and repetition. Keeping it up-to-date, fresh, true to your brand, these are the things that build success. Personal branding is something that takes time, but the payoff later comes in business and career opportunities you never thought possible.

The best single tip for all of your communication – for people in business and the professions – is to come up with three words that define your personal brand – describing a skill set or attitude or even community involvement. This might involve changing the way you see yourself, so you can then change the way others see you. Then it becomes a matter of being consistent, across all social networks that you are using.

So, with care, caution and an idea of your brand, put yourself out there – jump out of the box. It is one more of the building blocks that lead to your next promotion – and build your ability to lead people.

TEN SECRETS OF TOP "PERSONAL BRAND" COMMUNICATORS

How do the best professionals create a personal brand and advance their careers? What do leaders do differently once they have jumped out of the box of restricted view, and found courage to be everything they could be?

Many of these disruptive and innovative leaders have experience failure or setback – and then changed the way they see them self, and changing the way others see them, so their real leadership could develop and inspire others.

The first big leadership secret for most of us is to accept that in a modern world it is not enough to be very good at what you do – that's like sitting in the small box – whether your skill is a profession, science, IT, engineering, health, a trade, finance or consulting. In addition to being the best at what you do, you have to have an impact on those you serve and this comes down to improving your communication and leadership.

Here are ten secrets applied from the top "personal brand" communicators – the people who become truly disruptive, change agents and innovators:

PREPARED MESSAGES

Good branders always have a ready statement of where they are now, where they are going and how they will get there. They can deliver this message almost automatically.

ADDRESS PERCEPTIONS, NOT REALITY

Brand builders know that what people think of you holds the key to your future. You can do better at this by liking people more, listening to others asking lots of questions.

KNOW THEMSELVES

Good personal brand builders can sum up themselves and their company in a few sentences. Liking their organisation, they know their organisation well. Can you do that?

EXPLAIN CAPABILITIES

Good communicators can list their strengths and capabilities, as if it is a recorded message. This includes what you've done and where you are going.

COMPLEX TO THE SIMPLE

Successful professionals are great at summing up complex things in simple language. The more technical their knowledge, the simpler their language.

USE THE 5W'S

The best answer the 5W's in the first sentences of a discussion or meeting – Who, What, Where, When and Why? (and sometimes they add a "how")

AVOID CLICHES

Good brand communicators are down to earth and practical.

ASK QUESTIONS

The best business communicators are always asking questions. They interested and in- quisitive, because they like people.

ALWAYS – A PURPOSE

There is rarely any small talk for the top brand builders – they are always "on message". They are not backward in making purposeful statements.

MAKE AN IMPACT

Top brand builders can grab the audience, large or small, largely through their passion and belief – then they develop their message and close with impact.

My final piece of leadership branding advice is based on the best I have met in India and in the west – build your leadership on strong values such as honesty, generosity and patience and then your personal communication is seen as truth, friendship and inspiration. You will need courage to do this, because everyone who is stuck like you in a very small box fails to see the connection between very good personal values and personal success – you can only see this connection by breaking out of that box of self-imposed limitation.

CREATING THE MIND OF SUCCESS

Another "soft skill" you will not find in other soft skill books and courses – the great skill of building the mind of success. Actual success follows creating the mind of success. The mind of non-success or even of failure is the kind of mind that is stuck in a small box, afraid of the world, lacking the courage to make real connection and become outstanding communicators.

Our focus is on global communication skills based on values and the mind of success. Start now on the path to better global communication skills – the path to promotion and leading people. By making a beginning on the mind of success, you will find your leadership – changing the way you see yourself and the way others see you. This is the only way out of the small box of fear, anxiety, restriction and lack of success.

Greek philosopher, Epictetus, cautions us that the change we seek will not happen overnight: "Nothing great is created suddenly, any more than a bunch of grapes or a fig. If you tell me that you desire a fig. I answer you that there must be time. Let it first blossom, then bear fruit, then ripen." That is a key message – your impatience can be a negative. And he helps us adjust to the inevitable obstacles we will face: "It's not what happens to you, but how you react to it that matters."

If you put pressure on yourself to be an immediate success, you are likely to fail. As Indian cricketer Sachin Tendulkar said: "I always had a dream to play for India but I never let it put pressure on me." One way he avoids being overcome by pressure is: "I am not thinking too far ahead, just want to take it one thing at a time." Even in the heat of the game, he is thinking of the now rather than the end of the match: "I want to give my six hours of serious cricket on the ground and then take whatever the result."

It can be very useful every day to:

1. Revisit your plans and decide what action is needed now to make progress

2. Monitor the mind, ensure it can focus on the task at hand
3. Find inspiration from leaders and mentors who can go with the flow
4. Look at familiar things in a different way – taking nothing for granted
5. Be excited by whatever you are doing today, and do it to the best of your ability

Kumar Mangalam Birla is the Chairman of The Aditya Birla Group and a man of significant standing in India. He is a Director of the Central Board of Directors of the Reserve Bank of India, a member of the Prime Minister's Advisory Council on Trade and Industry, and Chairman of India's Board of Trade. He is dedicated to the 'melting pot' as a great asset, believing that heterogeneity helps transformation, and he expressed it using cricketing analogies: 'You need the fast bowlers, the spinners and the good wicket keepers just as much as the pinch hitters to become a winning team.'

Birla is above all a symbol of what is healthy in India's business leadership today. He has a simple view of leadership: "It is about building the highest levels of empathy, without compromising on fairness and running a popularity contest. So, the first lesson is that the process of change is perhaps 90 percent about leadership and only ten percent about managing." He takes this vision onto a global stage: "Our efforts in this area have been directed at building not an 'Indian manager who works internationally' but a 'global manager who happens to be Indian'."

Birla also counsels leaders to look after 'the mind', when most in the west think it is enough to look after the profits. He says: "Leaders must have the ability to mind your mind, which means quickly recognising when one is wrong and changing track accordingly. Also, far from being egocentric, they should have a great sense of humility."

He takes this concept of leadership even further with a dedicated focus on people: "Leadership is all about plugging in to the minds and hearts of people. It is about rallying them around to a compelling and exciting vision of the future. It is about upping the imagination of the organisation. It is about encouraging a spirit of intellectual ferment and constructive dissent so that people are not bound by the status quo, and mavericks are given space and free play." He also accepts that business, like life, can be about contradictions and paradox. That, for example, a leader at the same time seeks to minimise risk while encouraging entrepreneurship. Or making demands for work performance (long hours) while also investing in work-life balance, or monitoring quarter-by-quarter while also doing long-range planning.

This formula of living more in the now was taken up in the highly successful book, The Art of Happiness, by His Holiness and Dalai Lama and Dr Howard Cutler (more information at www.theartofhappiness.com) which puts forward a simple formula for happiness:

- The purpose of life is happiness
- Happiness is determined more by the state of one's mind than by external conditions, circumstances or events – at least once one's basic survival needs are met
- Happiness can be achieved through the systematic training of our hearts and minds, through reshaping our attitudes and outlook
- The key to happiness is in our own hands

It's good to sometimes reflect on the future, but when the future gets stuck in your mind you get stuck too. When thinking of the future gets us stuck, it is called "day dreaming". It becomes just another case of some idea, some thing or some person that we grip onto as if they are the very source of life, and in the process we stop.

In contrast, life does not stop, it is constantly changing. So every moment of day dreaming becomes a lost moment, we move one step further away from whatever it is we are aiming for.

Sometimes it is good to ask "What is the worst thing that could happen?" Say I cannot achieve my goal, is that so bad – or will the journey have been worth the effort? If I make some money but not great riches, have I really failed? If I lose everything, is that so bad if I am also a resilient, positive and action oriented person who can recommence building my life? Asking what is the worst thing that could happen can loosen our grip and help us realise just how resilient we can be.

It's like saying I would like to drive over there, but life is so changeable, the roads might be washed away, I might have to row a boat or help build a new bridge or whatever it takes. With an attitude such as "whatever it takes" dominating our mind, we get on with the task at hand and break out of the small box of restricted view. With just the end target in mind, we can get lost in regrets that obstacles have come in our way – this is like setting out on the path to success but because you are so focused on the end goal, your immediate actions put you back in the box.

It is no good thinking I will make progress once the obstacles have gone. Obstacles are our life, so find ways to overcome them.

Thinking too much about what we want destroys our peace of mind. People in the small box are always thinking about what they want, they are dreaming of what might be, but every time an obstacle comes along they hop right back into the box, because they have never worked hard on creating peace of mind. It is this peace of mind that makes us more effective right here and now, giving us a chance to reach our potential.

UNDERSTAND THE IRONY OF DISRUPTIVE, INNOVATIVE LEADERSHIP – BASING SOFT SKILLS ON GENEROSITY AND TOLERANCE

What kind of mindset do you need for good communication? What leads to that promotion? Which attitudes make us a good leader?

Many people see leadership as being forceful, impatient and unrelenting – driving others to exhaustion and punishing those who fail to meet impossible demands. This is a common and mistaken view from within the small box of personal limitation.

But I have studied successful leaders in India and the west and come to a different conclusion – the very best leadership, the kind that is

draf

disruptive and innovative, is based on strong values such as honesty, generosity and patience. The best leadership communication is based on truth, friendship and inspiring others. In other words, there is a lot of generosity and tolerance in what good leaders do. These are the values and mindset that rocket you out of that small box and project you into the real world of opportunity and achievement.

This might mean you change your view of leadership – but only by changing the way you see yourself, and changing the way others see you, can your real leadership develop and inspire others. The first step out of the box of failure and disappointment is to change the way you see yourself.

The task of building an open and generous mind is not taught at university, but it is a sound basis for real leadership success. If you can build a generosity, curiosity and tolerance into your daily life, while remaining true to family values, people will come to see what you can do for them, and you will be taking steps to where you want to be. We all like and respect people who are generous, curious and tolerant.

Here are some guide posts as you begin a career, take on a new path or seek to build a completely new business.

- **Respect who you are:** As your life changes, if people see that you are true to yourself, to your family values and to your spiritual belief, you will gain their respect and their support.
- **Be generous with your time:** Sitting behind the desk just won't do much for you – good entrepreneurs are always giving their time to others. Join in those activities which are good, become part of worthy groups or clubs and do not forget to phone your family, friends and other people important to your life.
- **Share what you know:** Too many professionals keep wonderful information locked away in their brains. Find the right time to pass knowledge on to others – but don't get attached to them agreeing with you because this attachment makes you tense and defensive.
- **Use social media:** We can make valuable connections with people if we are careful and thoughtful about using social media such as blogs, facebook and twitter. But don't overdo it, and always think carefully about what you are putting on the internet – it is there forever.

- **Learn how to speak in public:** People who can make thoughtful speeches have credibility and impact, so it is important at the beginning to learn the art of public speaking. Remember, always be honest and direct, show respect, speak when the opportunity is right and acknowledge the right of others to hold different views.

- **Build your networks and contacts:** There are many others out there who are trying to get to your target audience, and not all of these are competitors. Start talking to potential allies and once you meet people keep in touch with them.

- **Write thoughtful notes, letters and emails:** Don't forget in this age of technology that a personal note or letter is powerful. If you are living away from home, speak to your parents regularly but also send them a letter – it will be well received. Do the same with work colleagues and business contacts.

- **Volunteer your skills:** Others in the community might benefit from your free time, perhaps helping those in need. Or it might be that your workplace needs a group to volunteer to organise some extra activity – be generous, volunteer! Do it with a good heart and no expectation of a return for you.

In this competitive world, you can sit around wishing things would happen – or you can get out there and enjoy the communication journey. It is also wise to be wary of success, for it too can play with your mind – as Microsoft's founder, Bill Gates, said: "Success is a lousy teacher. It seduces smart people into thinking they can't lose." In my view, the journey is best started with a generosity of spirit, an open mind and a tolerance of others. Remember the saying about it all starting "with a single step"? Tagore said "Everything comes to us that belongs to us if we create the capacity to receive it". Just like a boomerang – put out good things and you will get good things back. You can have a daily checklist:

1. Reflect on how others have accepted your mistakes and helped you learn from those mistakes
2. Speak kindly to someone who looks troubled or isolated
3. Offer to do that bit extra, even for no financial benefit

4. Listen carefully to others, do not be distracted
5. When you have a helpful idea, find the right time and right words to offer it

Whether your skill is a profession, science, IT, engineering, health, a trade, finance or consulting, the challenge remains the same – in addition to being the best at what you do, you have to have an impact on those you serve and this comes down to improving your communication and leadership.

NETWORKING IS THE WAY TO "PLANT TREES"

Warren Buffett is a man I identify with going out and "planting trees" – which is his expression for personal networking. He did say: "Someone's sitting in the shade today because someone planted a tree a long time ago." He is showing us that by getting out of our chairs, meeting people, building relationships, starting ideas, talking a lot, we do "plant trees" that grow into success – for others and for us.

Networking is the best way to "plant trees" and in my corporate communication business, one of the most frequently asked questions by executives is: "How can I improve my networking?" The world would be a better place if we all networked, especially in our neighbourhoods. Like most things in communication, networking is not new and it is hardly rocket science.

I have seen many exciting young graduates and professionals who never reach their potential because of their fear of networking, their discomfort in social situations, their avoidance of being vulnerable and opening themselves to real connection and communication. They remain firmly stuck in that small box of self-imposed limitations where things seem "safe" – and so they never see either disaster or opportunity coming their way. Both will come your way – both disaster and opportunity confront us all at some time, which is why jumping out of the box is your best personal form of risk management.

You will only network well if you find your inner leadership, thereby changing the way you see yourself and this changes the way others see you – these become the building blocks of personal confidence.

I urge you to become true "tree planters", getting out and meeting people, building relationships and you never know what might become possible. My seven tips for networking (for planting trees) come from the best corporate networkers, the leaders who really know how to "work a room" and make an impact at any event; you might be able to use these ideas in your area.

FOCUS, FOCUS, FOCUS

When you first start talking to someone (whether an old friend or someone you have just met) concentrate your focus totally on them. Stay "in the moment" with this one person.

BE PRECISE, BE BRIEF

The long-winded person or the vague (I'm not sure why I'm here, don't know where I'm going, what's happening?) person generally fail at networking. Why? Because everything they do or don't do suggests that you are not important. In networking, the best perceptions are created by being precise and brief when you meet people. You might need to have a one or two sentence standard opener, developed before you go to that community meeting, function or seminar.

OPEN UP, LIGHTEN UP

Being too serious about networking can make you less effective. After all, networking is just people getting to know people. It can help to open up about yourself; perhaps admitting a lack of understanding of some area. Being ready to laugh, smiling a lot are all encouraging signs for the other person, letting them know you are enjoying the chat.

SET AN AGENDA

The old expression "set the agenda" is just a corporate way of saying go along to a function or meeting with a specific goal in mind. This goal might be to meet a specific person, or to communicate a single message. It could be to collect six business cards before you leave. One successful journalist used to ask political leaders and corporate chiefs about their hobbies and turn the conversation to this specific interest. It had the benefit of putting these leaders at ease and adding a human dimension to the communication.

INTRODUCE PEOPLE

Once you become a little comfortable with networking, you will be more aware of opportunities to introduce people to others who might share an interest. Most of us react well to this. It shows that you genuinely care about that person.

DON'T PIN PEOPLE DOWN

Functions such as community gatherings, luncheons, seminars, conferences or after work drinks are not occasions for the hard sell. If you believe networking equates to "making a sale" or "finding a job", think again. Networking is about making a contact, ultimately making a friend.

ALWAYS FOLLOW UP

A few days after the event, send a message to everyone you met (that's why you'll need to collect those business cards). If you promised to find something out for a person, make the phone call and keep the promise. Keep the contact going, invite them to coffee or to lunch, treat the networking occasion as just the beginning.

If you are nervous before going to any public gatherings or meetings, you will find that going along with a plan (I will introduce myself to three new people) can take your mind off the nerves and make you a better networker. Networking is just a new word for building relationships, and good relationships start with communication. It all comes down to the art of "planting trees", something which leaders do with great enthusiasm in their quest for "the good life".

What is ruling your mind? It is important for us to know, because whatever is ruling the mind will be taking up most of our time and energy. Life is short, so let's hope this time and energy is well spent. A selfish or disturbed mind will stop you being a good networker.

Right now we can reflect – am I attached to my possessions, want more and would I really hate losing them or not getting more? This "gain and loss" mentality sees life as a scoresheet, with my identity found in things. Is this what you really want?

Or consider how much you want to be praised and approved of by others, compared to how desperately unhappy you become when receiving blame or disapproval. This "praise and blame" approach puts others in charge of your most precious asset – your mind.

Taking that mind further, we can cling to having a good image, having others thinking well of us and feel very nervous about any damage to our reputation – a "fame or disgrace" scorecard that comes to dominate our mind. Again, do we really want to place our happiness in the hands of others?

Or finally, do we see constant pleasurable ex-periences as the key to happiness, and feel deep resentment when taken ill or not having fun? This "pleasure or pain" approach is unrealistic when you consider how much can go wrong in the course of life.

It is great to have possessions, be praised, have a good reputation and plenty of pleasure – but when we put too much value on them, become desperate for them, they become just another way to disturb our state of mind.

A preoccupation with avoiding pain, gaining only praise, benefiting just oneself and thinking only of your own image – these are the mindsets that put you in the small box and come between you and success.

Living in this desperate way leaves our state of mind in the hands of others or of events – a high risk strategy. By reclaiming the mind, we can find balance and strength, regardless of what is actually going on. Balance and strength are two things which will put you front and centre for promotion, making you a better leader.

HANDLING COMMUNICATION DURING A CRISIS

If you want to make it to the top of build a successful business, you will need the skills to deal with a crisis – we all face crises, and real leaders are the ones who know how to deal with the challenge. The person who is stuck in the small box of failure and disappointment lives in constant fear of a crisis and when one hits – as they always do – this person has neither the skills nor the temperament to face up to the challenge.

A colleague was in the first day as senior Partner on a major project when he circulated all staff with a small sign: "Our reaction to events can be more important than the events themselves". His biggest fear was that a well-intentioned member of staff would do a "cover up" when something went wrong. The purpose of the sign was to let them all know that what we do about a mistake is more important than the mistake itself.

At a personal level, we hope to go through our careers without facing a crisis. But we should have a plan and a way of thinking ready for in case one hits. Almost every organisation or individual embroiled in a crisis did not see it coming.

It's worth looking closely at how you and members of your team react when something goes wrong. This can be a good test of your way of thinking. If a simple request from a customer or someone you report to has been somehow overlooked, do you put your hand up, admit the error and get on with fixing it? Or do you think you might keep quiet, processing the request late and hoping that nobody notices? If you have this thought for even a moment, it means you need to change the way you think. There is no stronger ally and no greater defence in times of difficulty than the ability to instantly "own up" to your contribution to the problem.

The approach of keeping things quiet occurs too often among businesses, mostly in those firms where internal communication is poor, and where the people at the top are feared rather than respected.

We know from business studies that many companies are damaged more by their reaction to a crisis than by the crisis itself. It is the same for the individual.

Some of the worst corporations react to a crisis by covering up; second they lash out at anyone and everyone; third they seek refuge in legal action, and; fourth, they forget to keep their best friends (their staff, customers) informed. By pretending there is no problem, they guarantee that it gets worse. Problems don't solve themselves; people do.

We would all know of individuals who lash out and are known for taking legal action when anything goes wrong; finishing up with less money than they started with and with tarnished reputations.

When good corporations face a crisis or a problem, they take these six steps and it is worth trying to engender this approach:

- Get the facts (the first casualty of war is the truth, and it sure disappears when we are angry or in crisis)
- Communicate action (people respect you if you act positively, even if at first you were wrong)
- Review stance and processes (take a look at yourself, do you have to change?)

- Take market soundings (ask others what they think)
- Change behaviour and practices (you will improve if you try to change)
- Get the new message across (work on positive communication)

Note how the bad corporation just lashed out in haste, while the good takes its time and considers the situation; this suggests that patience is the key.

Sometimes we face conflict, rather than a crisis. Conflict can escalate into a crisis, so it is important to have a personal approach to conflict. In most areas of working life, disputes and conflict do arise from time to time and can become a crisis. So what do you do about conflict?

Is there something underneath it all? An important first tactic is to explore the possibility that there are some deep problems within the office. There is a simple honesty to this approach that stands you in good stead.

Avoid "tit for tat" reactions. Yelling at someone increases the level of conflict. Just as bad is having a go at others behind their back, or using your position to ram something through when skillful communication would produce better long term outcomes.

Don't force an end to conflict. This might work short-term, but for real long-term resolution of group conflict, let the group work on the conflict. You can apply this at home too, especially with teenagers. A common mistake parents make is to lead by "instruction" instead of leading by discussion.

Crushing people today can ruin them for tomorrow. If one person is playing up, the best senior corporate executives know that simply crushing them might end the misbehaviour today, but the cost could be that the person leaves the group or makes a lesser contribution to the team. This can be quite a loss, so hesitate and think before you use heavy criticism to end conflict.

Resolving conflict harmoniously is not a matter of being weak or letting people walk all over you within the office. We all face tricky emotional situations (at home, school or work) when it is important to assert yourself. You will say "no" and mean it more often if you have made a prior decision to be strong. The best way to assert yourself is straight away. If, for example, you suspect there is a conflict brewing in the office, gather the right people together and talk about it; do not hesitate.

One further lesson from the corporate world is while being assertive and dealing with a problem situation, try to keep a steady, friendly gaze into the other person's or the group's eyes. Almost every communication-training program for senior executive places a lot of focus on eye contact. If you look at the ceiling, cover your mouth, look anxiously back and forth, you will be misunderstood, sowing the seeds for the next crisis.

But, what if you have lost your cool and need to apologise? If you have to deliver an apology, the first choice is how personal should you be? Face-to-face is the most personal, the most intimate. But we have many other ways to deliver messages today, including a phone conversation, a voice-mail message, a handwritten note, an email, a fax, some flowers or a box of chocolates.

Some people say that there is no match for the human voice, especially for sensitive messages. Others think an email is more caring and more polite, because it does not interrupt the receiver – it gives them a chance to read and think before responding.

Delivering an apology in several ways reinforces your sincerity and concern. You might say it in person, send some flowers and call later to see how things are; that's three steps back to normal relations.

There are no hard and fast rules on how to deliver an apology. The most important thing is to deliver it. Corporations have learned the hard way that pretending a problem will go away is the best way to turn a small problem into a major and costly disaster.

When things are harmonious and smooth, most of us can work well – even those stuck in the small box of restriction, caution, fear, separation and anxiety seem to do well when things are good. But the people who win promotion and become leaders are those who can manage any form of crisis, who thrive under difficulty and find a way through the maze of problems. These are the ones who jump out of the box. That is why your leadership needs to be based on strong values such as honesty, generosity and patience – and your personal communication based on truth, friendship and inspiring others.

ETHICAL SUPERVISION AND LEADERSHIP

So you are about to become a supervisor. Congratulations – an exciting time in your career. But this is not a step that is just about you, for it has a major impact on others – those you supervise, report to or collaborate with and more.

What is an ethical way to make decisions? How can you use ethical thinking as a leader? There is a very simple answer that might work for you – first ask if the action you are about to take will cause harm. Then, ask if the action you are about to take will produce good. Actions are rarely either purely harmful or helpful – so then it becomes your judgement of minimising the harm and maximising the good. This ethical decision making process can be used in every part of life – do no harm, act for the good or do as little harm as possible and act for as much good as possible.

The key to positive outcomes is your intentions. Good intentions will lead to good results – so this ethical basis is not just theory – it becomes a real action program.

Supervision is not just about skills and confidence – it quickly displays your ethical base. So, in addition to learning the skills so many other supervisors and managers have learnt, you need a clear ethical framework for your supervision approach. In this way, setting goals for the team and motivating them has a much more solid foundation.

I have talked about my own study of leadership in India and the west – including ethics – and my belief that your leadership should be ethically based on strong values such as honesty, generosity and patience, with your personal communication inspiring others because of your commitment to truth and friendship.

One of your first steps should be to gain a clear understanding of a team leader's position and responsibilities from those you will be reporting to. They will want to hear your ideas on team leadership but you should also seek their views on techniques to get the best out of your team.

For example, most experienced managers will have managed difficult people and challenging situations, so why not benefit from their experience? They can also contribute to your approach to effective personal time management, which is also closely linked to your growing ability in delegation of skills.

As you go down the path of supervision and leadership, you will gain confidence in asking some of the really hard questions – Are your staff members satisfied with your leadership? Do you have a good working relationship with all members of the team? Does the team share a common goal and vision?

Bookstores are overflowing with books on leadership, but there are some core elements to guide you – and never forget you are part of a management team and others can show you the way. Use their knowledge and experience, trust their guidance, ask for their leadership as you lead others. And then, build some of these ingredients into your own approach:

INVOLVE THE TEAM IN THE VISION

Your team is looking to you for guidance and inspiration – so it is vital that you describe the vision for your team (no matter how small it might be) and you then repeat this vision as often as possible, using different approaches. You can set the vision out one on one, in groups, by email, in casual conversations and more. It works best if you challenge team members to show how they understand the vision and their role in it. Every good leader I have met has been able to communicate the vision in a clear way so the team knows it. In this way, you ensure the whole team is heading in the right direction.

MOTIVATE OTHERS

As a supervisor, you can now see that you have followers. These followers look to you for motivation, and you do this best by lots of encouragement and always praising effort that is contributing towards the vision. Often you will forget to do this, but good leaders are masters of feedback. You do not have to be a great orator – just a genuine and ethical person who wants everyone to do their best. That is enough.

SET THE EXAMPLE

As a supervisor or leader, you have become the benchmark for others. If you do not put in the effort, nor will they. If you cut corners, they will too. Whatever you do now, others are really watching and they will follow your lead. So, set the best example. Live by your values, Share your values. Make sure your actions are consistent with your words – sometimes known as "walk the talk".

PRODUCE RESULTS

If you break down tasks into small components, then you and the people who follow you can see what has been achieved and what is ahead. This is about putting the focus onto results. Too often, team members see the challenges as just too big. The supervisor and leader can help the team by breaking this challenge into manageable sections. Then, as each bit is done, make sure the team knows that good results have been achieved.

BUILD YOUR OWN TEAM

Gradually, you will be in charge of who joins your team and it is vital you find the right people. Within the group, you will develop a central team who are your best followers and who – in their way – show future leadership possibilities. Within this group, you should build trust and confidence, as well as a clear understanding of how the combined strengths and weaknesses make up the successful group.

BECOME AN ACTION PERSON

Have a bias for action: Leaders make things happen. You now have to do this. Decide in any situation what needs to be done, and then take action to move your team forward. This is what the team is looking for you to do. And always, when you are not sure what action is right, consult those you report to, talk to mentors, ask other leaders – it is the best way to add to your already great potential.

To build this approach to leadership will probably mean you change the way you see yourself – finding your inner strength and wisdom – so that others will then change the way they see you.

MASTERING THE LEADERS ART OF PERSUASION

To get more of what you want, including personal success and good friendships, you will have to improve in the art of persuasion. To persuade others means you have the courage to stand for something. From the viewpoint of the small box of self-imposed limitations, of fear, restriction and failure, we can look at great leaders with only envy. But when we break out of the box, we see leadership and persuasion as challenging us to be courageous enough to be the person we could really be.

A common mistake is that people link persuasion with "hard sell". Yet when we look at the best leaders – those who disrupt and innovate – we can see that their approach is not hard sell.

Persuasion is really a matter of give-and-take, so you do need to be prepared to compromise. The most persuasive leaders communicate strong values such as honesty, generosity and patience – and their communication is founded on truth, with an attitude of friendship. That is why we find these leaders so inspiring.

We can find inspiration here from the great Nelson Mandela, who committed himself to peaceful persuasion rather than violence: "If you talk to a man in a language he understands, that goes to his head. It you talk to him in his language – that goes to his heart." Mandela also had great advice for dealing with those who might be against you: "If you want to make peace with your enemy, you have to work with your enemy. Then he becomes your partner."

It is also a mistake to confuse argument or forceful announcements with persuasion. You might argue your position beautifully, but it is only part of the story and you need also to create empathy with others, connect with them and create some emotion. Mother Teresa urges us to bring this quality of mind close to home: "It is easy to love the people far away. It is not always easy to love those close to us. It is easier to give a cup of rice to relieve hunger than to relieve the loneliness and pain of someone unloved in our own home. Bring love into your home for this is where our love for each other must start."

Burma's great champion of democratic persuasion, Aung San Suu Kyi, had this to say in the beginning of her well known "Freedom From Fear" speech: "It is not power that corrupts but fear. Fear of losing power corrupts those who wield it and fear of the scourge of power corrupts those who are subject to it."

Sir Richard Branson, Founder of Virgin, is a great persuader and leader, but his view is that you have to be in the action in order to lead: "Nobody respects a leader who doesn't know how to get his hands dirty and innovate personally. The trick is in striking the right balance between empowering your staff and being an example for them to follow." Branson is well known for his love of parties and fun – and he has a reputation as a great delegator within his businesses. His philosophy is: "…even when you're successful, it is vital that you don't solely lead your company from a distance. Walk the floor, get to know your people. Even though I don't run Virgin companies on a day-to-day basis any more, I still find it crucial to get out and about among our staff."

Persuasion among top executives is also rarely a "one shot" effort. Like so many parts of communication, you need to be prepared to try, try again. It can be slow and difficult, but it is worth the effort. It helps you move forward and upward.

In the corporate "art of persuasion" you can learn from five main elements:

CONNECT EMOTIONALLY

Emotion works two ways in persuasion. First, we need to show our commitment to whatever we are advocating (ourselves, community, or cause, careers, organisational change), so that people know we feel it in our heart, mind and gut. But second, you also need to be aware of the emotional state of the people you are trying to persuade. Advertising legend Leo Burnett described it this way: "Anyone who thinks that people can be fooled or pushed around has an inaccurate and pretty low estimate of people". Knowing this, you can adjust your message and tone to suit your audience. Like corporate communication, it becomes a matter of knowing yourself and knowing your target. To those who feel women are better or worse than men in any of these areas, look for inspiration in this quote from feminist writer Robin Morgan: "Women are not inherently passive or peaceful. We're not inherently anything but human."

COMMON GROUND

Without common ground, you will not persuade. For example, if mistakes have been made you do not find common ground by publicly blaming others. As car maker Henry Ford said: "Don't find fault. Find a remedy". This is great reminder to be positive and find common ground. Your messages need to be framed so they appeal strongly to the people you want to persuade. You will only do this if you know what they are thinking, which means you have to listen to them. A common mistake is to focus totally on your own message, leaving no room for feedback, increasing the risk that your messages miss the target. The best corporate persuaders have all had a keen interest in others and the ability to listen, and this will work for you, too.

BE DRAMATIC

Facts do not excite people. We all look for some spark, some fizz in the message, so you will need to increase your presentation skills. Your messages become stronger if you tell them through anecdotes, personal reminiscences, stories and authoritative sources. Even the use of quotations can add some drama to your comments. The master of the quote was President John F. Kennedy, President of the USA in the early 1960's – "Our most basic common link is that we all inhabit this planet. We all breathe the same air. We all cherish our children's future. And we are all mortal."

Inspiration to "have a go" can be found in the life of leading American actress, Jane Fonda, who had many hurdles to overcome: "I grew up feeling that I wasn't good enough, and that no-one would love me unless I was perfect. But no-one's perfect, we're not meant to be perfect. We're meant to be complete. But it's hard to be complete if you're trying to be perfect, so you kind of become disembodied. And I spent a lot of my life that way."

CREATE CREDIBILITY

If you have credibility you can be persuasive. Generally, the corporate scene is no different from our lives; credibility comes from being good at what you do, being reliable and trustworthy and by building good relationships. Once you have credibility, hang on to it. For it is easy to lose. As

American investment guru Warren Buffett said: "It takes 20 years to build a reputation and five minutes to ruin it. If you think about that, you'll do things differently." This point was reinforced by GE legend Jack Welch who claimed the best way to protect reputation and credibility was to "Be candid with everyone". This point was developed even further by Sir Ninian Stephen, Governor-General of Australia 1982-1989, when he said: "...three main components of leadership: mastery of the subject-matter, ability convincingly to articulate the particular course of action required and a fervent belief in its correctness."

BUILD TEAMS

Team players and team builders are our favourite people – so the tendency of Gen Y towards collaboration and engaging with peers is a great potential strength. We like these team players, and we listen to them. We allow them to persuade us. Every time you are in a group setting, try to contribute something positive, that will make the group feel good. Being in teams also helps you learn to negotiate conflict, a good launching pad for persuasion.

The art of persuasion is something you can learn throughout life. You will never perfect this art, so keep learning. The more you can create a genuine interest in and caring attitude for others, the more you will be liked and trusted by them. Fear, on the other hand, keeps you isolated from people and firmly on the road to failure. Communication is all about liking and understanding people, creating the highway to success. If you communicate well, there is much less chance of being overlooked, much greater chance of moving towards a better relationship. But it all comes back to the simplicity of being a good, honest person, and thinking of others so that, in the words of Mother Teresa, "Let no one ever come to you without leaving happier."

The 19th century President of the USA, John Quincy Adams, said: "If your actions inspire others to dream more, learn more, do more and become more, you are a leader." That is, it is up to you. Like happiness, leadership is a choice.

In the process, we need to be able to follow those who inspire and lead us, so we can then go on to inspire and lead others. As the Greek philosopher Aristotle advised: "He who has never learned to obey cannot be a good commander." To lead and inspire others, you will sometimes need great courage – Martin Luther King Jr, champion of civil rights in America, knew from his own experience: "The ultimate measure of a man is not where he stands in moments of comfort, but where he stands at times of challenge and controversy." Leaders are always being watched by those they lead, which means your ethics are on show at all times. The great explorer of Africa, Albert Schweitzer, said: "Example is not the main thing in influencing others, it is the only thing."

Do not lose sight of your potential. You can have an impact. Your life will have real meaning if you act. Jump out of the box of self-imposed limitation. Pioneering anthropologist, Margaret Mead, provides the inspiration: "Never doubt that a small group of thoughtful, concerned citizens can change world. Indeed it is the only thing that ever has." I also keep reflecting on how "the good life" can be found in that quote from Mother Teresa, "Let no one ever come to you without leaving happier."

MAKING A STRONG SPEECH

I have sat through more bad speeches than good, so I am going to scare you right up front – there are many ways to ruin a good speech and most of us have been guilty of some of these. Poor public speaking, even in small groups, will hold your career back.

Here are some of the major pitfalls:

WHAT IS THE POINT?

A bad speech never lets us know what it is all about and our mind keeps asking "what is the point?" Good speakers even ask the question for the audience – so, what is my main point here? Having got our interest, they provide the answer.

LOTS OF FACTS

Too much information, too many facts, too many

numbers just eventually overcomes the audience who cannot remember any of them. Better to use a few key statistics and repeat them a few times – that way we will remember.

BADLY TOLD JOKES

Good jokes badly told are a real put off for the audience and it is better not to tell any jokes at all unless you are certain that they work. When in doubt, throw the joke out. But if you can tell a joke, remember the "rule of three" – always have three on the one subject, because they might not laugh at the first but they will at the second or third.

HEAD DOWN

If the speaker is head down, with eyes on the page and not making eye contact with us, it really creates a barrier between speaker and audience. As humans, we crave some eye contact. So, speak up and out, make occasional eye contact, project your voice, be positive and you will have an impact.

ON AND ON AND ON

When the speech is in monotone and the flow of power points is regular and predictable, we, the audience, simply cannot tell what is important and what your main point is, let alone what it is you want us to do. So, mix up the pace, mix up the tone – and when you come to an important point raise your voice and say "Now this brings us to my most important point…"

ALL OF A SUDDEN, IT IS OVER

Many speakers just finish and that is that. It is awkward for us as an audience – we are not sure what to do, should we applaud, is it over, what is happening? Much better to introduce your last two or three sentences by stating "Now, in conclusion, my main points today are…" and then always close with a friendly "Thank you".

Now, there are times when all you have to do is update a group on a project – that is, the purpose of the presentation or speech is to inform. By deciding which facts and which details are really important, you will help the audience follow your information – and there is less need for calls to action or motivation. But do it well, introduce some power point but not too much, and run through the main stuff because other details can generally emerge in discussion or via question.

But, when your speech or presentation is part

of leadership, it has to persuade and motivate, and that needs a different approach. This kind of speech can express passion and emotion, but it is always useful to return to logic, reasoning or even to quote others from history or thought who might support your case. If using a quote, it is good to put it on power point so people can read while you talk.

For speech making there is actually a sequence to follow when you want to motivate an audience, so you should follow these five steps:

- Attention – get their attention which in my language means opening with impact
- Need – establish why this is important
- Solution – present a legitimate and credible solution to the situation
- Support – back up your solution with statistics or quotes from others and highlight the pitfalls of other approaches
- Action – call for audience action, ask people to respond and outline how they should act

I also strongly recommend that speakers ask questions – often these are questions the audience is asking too, so they are grateful to hear it from the speaker. Even the occasional "So, what is my main point here" is a good attention device. Some of the best are:

- What is my major point on this topic? Allows you to reinforce the importance of the topic to the audience
- Are there examples? Allows you to add examples to your point of view
- But what does this mean for you? Reinforce what it means to them and tell the audience what you want them to do. This is a great finishing technique for any speech or personal presentation

Here are some further tips to help you with presentations and speeches:

NERVOUSNESS

Every speaker feels some nerves so you are not special in that sense. But trying to fight nerves never works, so learn to accept them. Good preparation and rehearsal will reduce your nerves, and knowing exactly what you want to say at the beginning can get you off and running. I also think it helps to really have an attitude of liking your audience and feeling that you want to help them as best you can.

PREPARATION

I am often praised for impromptu speeches but I can share a secret with you – I am always prepared, at least for part of what I want to get across. Preparation is the key and you should go through your draft and challenge what is there – is it persuasive?

YOU KNOW THE TOPIC

Generally the reason you are doing a speech or presentation is because of your knowledge – so you know the topic better than your audience does.

MEMORISE OPENING LINES

If making a significant speech to a larger group, it can help your confidence if you have memorised the opening lines.

FOCUS ON THE AUDIENCE

Nothing reduces nerves more than placing your focus on the audience, not on you. The best secret here is to pick out two or three people in different parts of the room and initially move your eye contact from one to the other. Gradually, you can branch out from there.

LENGTH

Plan a speech that is shorter than the allotted time. Audiences will be grateful and you will be seen as well prepared and straight to the point – good leadership qualities.

PERSONAL

The audience really loves to hear a little about you so telling personal stories and anecdotes can be a good small inclusion in a speech – but not too many and not too long.

ASK QUESTIONS

A great way to break up a speech and regain the attention is to ask simple questions as you finish one section and are about to start another. A simple, "So what does this mean for us?" will work well to transition to your next point and regain attention. Some people like to start a speech and this can be very powerful but you need to have a strong and relevant question.

BREATHE EASY

Taking too many deep breaths can get far too much oxygen into your brain and increase nerves, so my approach is instead of sucking in air when nervous, shift your focus to a long and relaxed exhale of air. It feels good and slows things down.

PAUSES

It is Ok to pause and be quiet for a while. No need to rush, silence is Ok, it certainly gets attention and it can be good to follow a pause with a sharp question.

VOLUME

Some people say speak loudly but the real secret of good speechmaking is to vary your volume. An increase in volume is good for major points or key questions and it gets the audience back on track with you.

HANDS

Keep hands still and out of pockets. Constantly moving hands are distracting, while hands in pockets looks like you do not care much. But do use hands for emphasis. Avoid folding your arms or fidgeting with pens and so on.

MANNERISMS

Avoid ricking back and forth on your feet – best to have a rehearsal in front of a friend or a mirror and you might be surprised by the distracting mannerisms you adopt.

EYE CONTACT

Does not have to be constant, but on a regular basis you will need to shift your gaze to the audience and try to make specific eye contact with individuals.

POWER POINT

A great aid to speaking when used well – but when there are too many numbers or too many words or in fact when the whole speech is on the power point, it comes between you and the audience. A few numbers is better than many. A few words are better than a page full of words. Try not to turn away from the audience to look at the screen – you should have a small computer screen in front of you so you can see what they are seeing on the big screen.

If you continue to say "I am no good at public speaking" then chances increase that you will be no good. It also means you will not try to be better. Every good speaker has tried and tried, falling over and getting back up to have another go. You could do the same, but the only way to start is to jump out of the box that says you cannot do it.

REMOVING OBSTACLES TO COMMUNICATION AND SUCCESS

Obstacles, it turns out, are in many ways what life is all about. You might think success and happiness will come when all these problems are out of the way – but in reality life just keeps presenting problems. Our level of happiness and success comes from our ability to deal with problems and obstacles. This is what I mean about the negative habit of living life as if sitting in a "safe" box of self-imposed limitation and restriction. Only by jumping out of that box do we find the courage to deal with whatever life throws at us, to be truly resilient and able to bounce back time and again.

There are ten major barriers – mostly caused by our mindset – coming between us and reaching our potential:

1. Not living in the "now" – means mind is overloaded and emphasizes whatever it is that troubles us about past or future. Life is not the past or the future, and if we are thinking about them we miss life as it happens. Many thoughts about past or future actually create emotions and anxiety. How to live in the now? Training the mind is the answer.

2. Expecting things to go our way all the time is like living in a "fools paradise". This is attachment. "They" should understand me, or do this, or that. This view means we will never be happy and never be effective problem solvers.

3. Low self-esteem creates an immense blockage between you and your potential. We are good at self-criticism and this becomes stressful, also means we look at life fearfully because do not believe we can cope.

4. When we are so desperate for success, we can be really hurt by not getting what we want – yet inevitably there will be times

when we do not get what we want. The solution is to be ready for it, be strong when it occurs. If we desperately seek something and the seeking is stressful then the not getting is painful.

5. Delaying happiness (after I get my degree, after I get married, when the boss understands me, when I get a new car) means we do not face up to life as it is now. We will put up with bad conditions and stress now because we will be happy later on – but later on never comes. Choosing to be happy now instantly reduces this stress and makes us better at finding solutions.

6. Always looking "outside" for happiness is a way of never allowing your potential to shine. Believing others can make me happy or jobs can make me happy or things can do it leads to more craving, clinging, stress, because it does not deliver. Happiness is a state of mind.

7. Taking our mind for granted (it is wonderful) means it never grows or adapts – you stay stuck in a rut. We look after the body – feed it, clean it, train it and we need to do the same for the mind. Nothing in the universe compares to the

mind, and our whole experience is mind made, so look after it. Otherwise, we are seeing life in two dimensions – good and bad, like and dislike, past and future etc and this itself is stressful.

8. Grasping, craving, feeling desperate about the future are recipes for stress and failure. We can be driven by three feelings – pleasant, neutral and unpleasant. This means we grasp at the pleasant and try to drive away the unpleasant. It is more realistic to accept reality – icecream might be nice on a hot day, but too much makes you sick.

9. Ignoring the harsh reality of life – what is born dies, what is created changes, impermanence and death – means we never expect a setback and are shocked when it occurs. A mind in shock is not going to find a way forward. Alternatively, if we are more aware of the inevitability of death, we choose to live better now. We live as if life and things are permanent and then we grieve for every little change.

10. Expecting life to be a bed of roses, when it does incorporate suffering, is like going for a swim but never having learnt to swim.

Birth, sickness, aging, death, not getting what want, being parted from what have, confronting what we don't like – this is life. The secret is in going with the flow, rolling with the changes, taking opportunities and being adaptable.

Future employers want to be able to see your true potential – but if you cannot see it yourself, how can you expect them to find it? There is one major thing employers want – this was summed up in the Financial Times "What do employers want? In two words: soft skills."

Start now on the path to better global communication skills – the path to promotion and leading people. The starting point is in your mind – the mental box that limits you – so find your leadership – change the way you see yourself and you will change the way others see you.

MANAGING AND COMMUNICATING WITH DIFFICULT PEOPLE

Do other people pull you down into some kind of a den of discord and disharmony? Do you ever wished you could make instant change to difficult people? Managing difficult people is really about learning how to get along with people that you probably do not even like.

Remember that the experts say "misery likes company" – that is, miserable people seek out other miserable people. This is what I mean by living in the box of limitation and restriction. On the other hand, optimism and happiness and success are contagious, so why not mix with people who will infect you with these wonderful things?

For a manager or leader, it is these people skills that can build success where others might fail. It is easy to say we should just rise above any negative feelings, but in truth this is a learned skill. The difficulty is not just found in staff – it can be among customers or suppliers. Customers today are becoming more demanding and less tolerant and they want their issues resolved "now". It is possible to learn skills that reduce your stress and allow you to respond effectively and positively to difficult people.

ANALYSIS

A good starting point is to know why people are so difficult. For example, we all have different personality types and it is worth knowing these to help you then understand the difficult person you are dealing with. All personality types can be influenced and dealt with in a way that is good for you and good for business.

MOTIVATION

Knowing the various triggers that can make people difficult is also a valuable management and leadership tool. For each personality type, there will be certain situations that cause aggression and negativity in them. By knowing the triggers, you can do something to avoid them occurring and you can repair things when they have led to confrontation. There are also certain aggressive and assertive behaviour patterns – knowing these can help you deal with them.

LISTENING

Whatever the personality type and whatever the situation trigger, listening is the most valuable way to start. This can be a learned approach, because for many of us our first instinct is to be aggressive in return or to try for a quick fix – when the other person is not ready for a fix. By listening and observing, you are actually collecting facts and finding options for dealing with the situation. In many cases, difficult people feel that nobody listens to them, so your approach will be a pleasant change.

CONTROL

Control of self is a key ingredient in dealing with difficult people and when you are in control of self your body language becomes an asset. When you are out of control, your body language could be aggressive or contemptuous without you even being aware of it. An open and interested body language only comes from being under control.

EMPATHY

Communication works best when we have self-respect and respect for the other party – even for the difficult person. Like listening, empathy should be one of your first goals well before you work out a solution. Empathy is simply a platform for shared understanding and also opens the possibility of agreeing with different viewpoints. This agreement can become your pathway to resolution.

QUESTIONS

A great technique to demonstrate listening and empathy – while also stopping you reacting and speaking too soon – is to ask questions of the difficult person. Open ended questions are ones that cannot be answer with a mere "yes" or "no" and these work best for you.

EXPLANATION

At some stage, you will need to explain the situation so the difficult person has a chance to become productive or to become a buyer again. You will need to move them a little your way, after establishing listening and empathy. In tense situations, explanations need to be calm and simple.

CONFIDENCE

By maintaining a confident attitude – even while initially listening – you will demonstrate this self-control and self-awareness to the difficult person. Keeping your balance and seeing a way through – these are great signs of managerial and leadership skill.

The people who are considering your next promotion will be considering how you handle difficult people – so it is worth developing your skills with people you just do not normally relate to. You can become a problem solver, rather than become overwhelmed by the problem. You can interact effectively even with the most disgruntled and difficult individuals.

Your success will be based on communication and decisions that reflect strong values such as honesty, generosity, patience, truth, friendship and inspiring others.

LISTENING, COMMUNICATION AND LEADERSHIP

Some of the world's best leaders have a great interest in people – you can see them, leaning forward, listening intently to what someone is saying. This is one outcome of the value of generosity – giving your complete attention to the other. On the other hand, sitting in the box of self-imposed limitation means you find very few if any people interesting, cynicism and negativity thrive in the box and you make no effort to listen deeply to others.

One major path to winning promotion is to work on your listening skills, and one proven way to lead others is by becoming a better listener. To "listen deeply" is to break out of the box and open to others.

Listening intently and deeply is about your mindset – Indian philosopher, Krishnamurti (1895-1986) can be a great source of inspiration and placed great importance on listening, and lamented: "If we try to listen we find it extraordinarily difficult, because we are always projecting our opinions and ideas, our prejudices, our backgrounds, our inclinations, our impulses; when they dominate we hardly listen to what is being said."

So the biggest obstacle to the art of conversation is the rise and fall of our thoughts. In the box of limitation, we are thinking all the time – thinking and not doing, thinking and not connecting. These thoughts stop us listening, and without listening how can we communicate? American management guru Peter Drucker also said that too often we raise important topics at the wrong time and place, with zero positive results: "The really important things are said over cocktails and are never done."

Alice Duer Miller was a writer, poet and one of the early advocates for empowerment of women, and she pointed out: "People love to talk but hate to listen. Listening is not merely not talking, though even that is beyond most of our powers; it means taking a vigorous, human interest in what is being told us. You can listen like a blank wall or like a splendid auditorium where every sound comes back fuller and richer." Her point was picked up by Gilbert Amelio, President and CEO of National Semiconductor Corp: "Developing excellent communication skills is absolutely essential to effective leadership.

The leader must be able to share knowledge and ideas to transmit a sense of urgency and enthusiasm to others. If a leader can't get a message across clearly and motivate others to act on it, then having a message doesn't even matter. Leaders who make it a practice to draw out the thoughts and ideas of their subordinates and who are receptive even to bad news will be properly informed. Communicate downward to subordinates with at least the same care and attention as you communicate upward to superiors."

American General Colin Powell: "The day soldiers stop bring you their problems is the day you have stopped leading them." Lee Iacocca famously said: "You can have brilliant ideas, but if you can't get them across, your ideas won't get you anywhere." And the dangers of not communicating well were vividly described by C. Northcote Parkinson: "The void created by the failure to communicate is soon filled with poison, drivel and misrepresentation."

Chinese philosopher, Lao Tzu has great perspective: "Silence is a source of great strength."

Stephen Covey, author of 7 Habits of Highly Effective People, wrote: "Seek first to understand, then to be understood." My Grandmother was a great listener, but with a moral edge: "If you can't say something nice, say nothing". This kind of reduced her art of conversation. She used to say a gossip talks about others, a bore talks about himself – and a brilliant conversationalist talks about you. To encourage us six siblings to listen, grandma would say: What are those things on the side of your head for? Why do you have two ears and one mouth? Good point gran.

What is the least effective way to respond to the other person? Assuming we are not completely lost in our own thoughts, the least effective version of the art of conversation is to respond to the other person in one of three ways – first, by probing for more of what *we want to know*; second, by bringing our autobiography into it (you tell me about breaking your arm yesterday, I recount my fall thirty years ago), and third, and this one is especially for we men, we like to give advice. This is not real listening.

Why does the art of conversation matter at all? Because conversation is one of the great ways we develop relationships; and it is through relationships that we can define ourselves and find meaning in this strange thing called life. Relationship grows through understanding, something we all want whether as individuals or leaders. A paradox is if you seek to understand, you will more easily be understood.

The key therefore, to getting started on the path to better conversations, is better listening. Christopher Morley, the American writer, put it so well: "There is only one rule for being a good talker. Learn to listen." This learning includes the ability to put thoughts aside as they arise and to thereby increase our awareness and openness to what is being said.

Listening is a magnetic and strange thing, a creative force. The friends who listen to us are the ones we move toward, and we want to sit in their radius. When we are listened to, it creates us, makes us unfold and expand.

Krishnamurti again: "I do not know if you have ever examined how you listen, it doesn't matter to what, whether to a bird, to the wind… to the rushing waters…in a dialogue with yourself…One listens and therefore learns, only in a state of attention, a state of silence, in which the whole background is in abeyance, is quiet; then, it seems to me it is possible to communicate." This is how we build a group of friends, whether in business or in life, and as an unknown writer put it: "To have a good friend is one of the highest delights of life; to be a good friend is one of the noblest and most difficult undertakings."

Mark Twain, with typical humour, wrote: "Friends are an aid to the young, to guard them from error; to the elderly, to attend to their wants and to supplement their failing power of action; to those in the prime of life, to assist them to noble deeds." 2,500 years ago, Greek philosopher Aristotle urged us: "Plant a seed of friendship; reap a bouquet of happiness."

Consider: why are the words "silent" and "listen" made up of exactly the same letters? Former USA President, Theodore Roosevelt said: "The most important single ingredient in the formula of success is knowing how to get along with people." Dale Carnegie was an expert in the field and he advised: "When dealing with people, remember you are not dealing with creature of logic, but creatures of emotion." Roger Enrico, Vice Chairman, Pepsico, in thinking about soft skills such as communication lamented: "the soft stuff is always harder than the hard stuff."

Compassionate Listening is an approach that grew out of the Society of Friends (Quakers) and a wonderful woman Gene Knudsen Hoffman who changed the way we think about peace-making and building bridges in communities. She found the roots of this listening in many spiritual practices and cultural traditions, as well as conflict resolution techniques. It is claimed that many scientific principles support the theory behind Compassionate Listening.

Some of the thinking behind Compassionate Listening is the following:

- Energy cannot be destroyed – only changed from one form to another (transduced).
- We can't save the world – the world is saving itself. We can align with those forces.
- For every action, there is an opposite and equal reaction.
- "A problem cannot be solved at the same level of thinking that created it. A larger perspective or deeper understanding is needed." Albert Einstein
- The whole is greater than the sum of its parts.
- Conflicts recycle, often in another form,

if the basic, underlying needs are not addressed.

- "There is a drive in living matter to perfect itself." Albert Szent-Gyoergyi, Nobel Prize winning biologist.

- "Perhaps every act of violence comes from an unhealed wound." Gene Knudsen Hoffman

- Within each problem is the key to its resolution. Within each wound is a pure essence seeking expression.

- Follow each conflict to its source. The sources of interpersonal conflicts are often unmet inner needs, competition for limited resources, and/or conflicts of values.

- Everyone who is part of the problem needs to be part of the solution. Each person involved is part of the whole.

- Listening is accepting but not necessarily agreeing.

- The opposing view is always valuable. Look for underlying commonalties to build solutions of mutual benefit.

- Compassionate Listening is not about satisfying curiosity or problem solving. It is about being present to another.

- In resolving conflict, focus on the problem – not the person.
- Humans are more alike than not. All humans share the same needs for security, safety, belonging, love, approval and fulfilment. These human needs cut through cultural differences and become the basis for common ground.
- What we have not resolved within is projected on others.

Within Compassionate Listening, there are five core beliefs or practices that make the listening deep and effective, and you will not find this thinking in most soft skills training programs or manuals. These are compassion, neutrality, respect, connection and speaking from the heart.

Compassion means the listener has a willingness to connect even when not in agreement with the other person. Neutrality is developing the role of the fair witness, remaining neutral in the conflict. Respect is respecting self and others, developing boundaries which protect yet include. Connection is listening with the heart, allowing divergence to exist and finding a deeper point of connection. Speaking from the heart is using different language, one that reflects a healing intention.

The actual wording of the Compassionate Listening organization for the five core practices of Compassionate Listening is:

- Holding Compassion for Oneself and Others
- Suspending Judgment
- Maintaining Balance in the Heat of Conflict
- Listening with the Heart
- Speaking from the Heart

By listening with compassion, you will become a more powerful peacemaker in the workplace, and this is greatly valued as disruption and division reduce productivity. You might also become the peacemaker in your family and community.

Compassionate Listening is a practice that reaches deep into the heart of discord or disconnection, teaching people to listen with a different "ear" to those around them. Its powerful tools help transform the energy of conflict into opportunities for understanding, intimacy at home, healthy relations, productive teamwork, and positive action. It is a practice that provides a road-map to what sages from all ages and cultures have taught: cultivating the wisdom of the heart is the key to real peace "from the inside out."

In the workplace, here are some suggestions on how to improve your listening and add to your managerial and leadership potential.

When Listening

- Early in the discussion, resist the temptation to try to "fix it" as quickly as possible, because the discussion and the listening could itself be part of the fix, which really only results from a clear commitment by all involved
- Have compassion for the speaker's situation
- Hear their story and make sure you do not try to relate it to your own. Too often the listening stops because we want to jump in with our own experience or our own story. You become an effective listener if you accept that this is not about you!
- Listen from both your heart and your head

- "Reflect" back what the speaker says to make sure you understand them correctly
- Avoid using confronting "why" questions because these can lead people back into the conflict
- Allow silence – most of us fear silence, but it can be a respectful space

When Speaking

- Speak warmly and openly (from the heart) about your own feelings and experiences, not your interpretation or judgment of the "other"
- Be aware of your body – if it becomes tense or body language is rigid, give yourself space to physically relax before speaking

I think it is useful to change your views about what listening is all about. Try to adopt the view that the purpose of listening is to be of service. The intention could go as far as healing or changing, but it is always to be of service. Once you have this intention, you will want to create a safe space in which the speaker can hear his or her own voice and present their story. Again, do not rush to solutions, but instead accept that the purpose of this type of session is not necessarily for problem-solving or to satisfy your curiosity – and that a big part of the solution is actually found in the act of patient listening.

Giving feedback to the other person is also a skill of listening – without it, the other person is not even sure they have been heard. My tips for good feedback include:

- Clearly state that the situation is a learning experience for all of us
- Thank and acknowledge the other person's courage for sharing with you
- Trust your honesty and combine it with empathy and compassion
- Be polite at all times and remember that the raw truth without compassion can seem abusive to the other person
- Check with the person that they have expressed it all and create extra opportunity for them to add thoughts or experiences
- Share a sense of appreciation and clearly state what the next steps are

Remember, some of the world's best leaders have a great interest in people – you can see them, leaning forward, listening intently to what someone is saying – and they do this because they have a generous attitude to others. Many of them had to learn to do this – they started like you cramped up in the isolated box of limitations, but they had the courage to jump out. Take a leap too – and you will find a key path to winning promotion is to work on your listening skills, and one proven basis for this is the value of generosity.

7 TIPS FOR WINNING SPEECHES AND PRESENTATIONS

1. Make a stand. Start your speech or presentation by showing passion, making your key point. For example, I sometimes start by thanking the speaker and then I say "The world's biggest selling business author, Stephen Covey, author of The 7 Habits of Highly Successful People, has written that communication is the greatest skill in life – it's a message I learned the hard way." The stage is set.

2. By all means use Powerpoint, but do not overuse it. The problem with many Powerpoint presentations is too much information, too many charts and poor content. You can use Powerpoint to show pictures instead of just facts and data.

3. Tell stories. Once you have decided the number of key points to make, think of a personal story or anecdote that relates to your key point. People do not want to hear "the 25 features of your new IT platform", but they will love a story about how you got started.

4. Stand tall, make friendly eye contact, walk free if you can, but never put your hand in your pockets. If you must stay at the lectern, just cling to it on occasions, not all the time. The microphones will pick your voice up even if you back off a little.

5. Don't apologise or tell us what you have to leave out. If time is short and you have to cut your speech short, just do it – the audience does not know what you were going to say anyway.

6. Give us a pause. By stopping, you keep our attention and reinforce that you have just made an important point. We love a short break (a few seconds is fine). I use counting to myself to put in the pauses, like this: "The world's biggest selling business author (pause, one, two three, while they wonder who it is), Stephen Covey (pause while they

take the name in) has written that 'communication is the greatest skill in life' (pause one, two, three, four, and if I can, pause even longer so they are desperate to hear what my next point is). It's a message I learned the hard way."

7. End with a stand. Let the audience know that you are about to make your concluding point, so they're ready for it. Then make the big statement that you used at the beginning to make a stand in the first place. Wrap it up with "I am grateful for your attention today. Thank you." Then you stand there and wait, because they will want to clap and it shows respect. Of course, in a business presentation you will need to find an informal way to finish, you will not expect applause but it is great to see people agreeing with you and enjoying what you have to say – and always show respect.

David Ogilvy, founder of global advertising agency Ogilvy & Mather, was one of the giants of the advertising industry last century. One of his themes was "be happy while you are living", and he identified this happiness as a key to effective communication and making new friends.

Before you can successfully lead and communicate with others, you need to really value them as human beings. They are not mere objects ready to hear your "pearls of wisdom".

The best way to value others is to reflect on how much they have done for you. Your parents took care of you, extended family helped out. They taught you how to speak, how to look after yourself, and they kept you away from danger. Your teachers passed on knowledge, perhaps spiced with motivation. Think of how important friends have been to you. On top of this, people you have never met have helped in different ways – planting and growing cotton for your clothes and so on. Complete strangers have grown the food we eat or made the roads we drive on. As we become aware of this, we more naturally feel a sense of gratitude, generosity and think more often of others rather than self.

Even someone who you do not get along with has given you something – an irritating opportunity to see how patient and tolerant you have become (or not).

Thinking this way, you can also develop a real sense of equality with others, realising how we all depend on each other. Further, we can consider that all beings are actually just like us –

they want a good life, they do not want to suffer and so on.

With this in mind, instead of thinking about "me" (when we are locked in the box of limitations, our favourite thinking topic is "me") we come to value others, and when we communicate we do it from their perspective, aware of what they are taking in and we can adapt our message to the needs of the moment. In that way, "they" do not have to search for the message, we make it easy for them.

This means your communication can be based on staying true to your values and heritage, while adapting to this changing world – very attractive features for those considering your promotion.

15 TIPS FOR YOUR JOB INTERVIEW

BE PREPARED

Be as prepared as you would be for a speech or presentation. Since the interview is mostly about you, make sure you know your strengths, weaknesses, potential and what you have achieved to date. Get used to meeting new people with a smile and over the time of the interview make eye contact with each member of the panel. You can do this with family at home, or with work colleagues.

RESEARCH THE EMPLOYER

You do not need to do a full analysis of the company or group, but it reflects well if you can show that you have done some homework.

This might also give you an opportunity to ask an informed question about future directions or challenges. You can find out as much as you can about the company through google – or go to annual reports, newspapers etc. Your research effort will stand out in the job interview – you will be seen as proactive, interested and astute.

DRESS LIKE THEY DO

Every company or organisation has its own culture and you will benefit from spending some time watching other employees come and go from your prospective employer's office. If you can, it is a good signal to dress appropriately to match the company culture – for example, many companies are now quite casual and you will not look like you fit if dressed very formally. Alternatively, casual clothing sends the wrong signal to a company that is traditional and formal. You can even ask the person who has arranged the interview for their advice. But if in doubt, always err on the side of conservative, formal business dress.

ARRIVE EARLY

They might keep you waiting but you will miss the job if you keep them waiting. Being punctual is a good sign of your interest and reliability. It is a good idea to know how to get there, exactly how much time you will need and so on. It is wise to be at the venue up to 30 minutes early, then go in to the reception about 5 minutes early.

BE ENTHUSIASTIC

Smile, walk up to your interviewers, do not hang back – be open, warm and friendly. It can be the "first impression" that lasts. Even in the reception show a friendly and warm approach – sometimes interviewers might seek an opinion or reaction from the receptionist or by personal assistants.

FEEL GOOD

While over confidence can be a negative, it is essential to feel good about yourself and confident that you will bring a lot to the job. This can be a subtle balance, but confidence is generally seen as a sign of success now and in future. You are who you are, so feel comfortable about "you" and really the rest is up to them. It is like "putting your best foot forward".

DON'T JUST TALK ABOUT YOU

Even though it might feel as if the whole process is about you, it is also important not to just talk about yourself. Mention colleagues or mentors who have impressed you, or ask questions that show you are genuinely interested in the company.

DO SOME PRACTICE

We all know some of the regular interview questions, so practice your answers to all the typical ones, such as "tell me about yourself", "what are your strengths" and "why are you looking for a new position?" The practice will help you to relax.

TREAT IT AS A CONVERSATION

Success in any business environment comes where all parties feel comfortable with each other and where a flowing conversation is taking place. This is not easy to achieve and will depend in part on your attitude to the interviewers – try to adopt an attitude of liking them, feeling as if they are old friends. Also remember that you never interrupt your interviewer – wait respectfully for them to finish whenever they speak. It helps the conversation if you can finish one or two answers with a polite "Do you mind if I ask a related question?"

BE CLEAR ON YOUR VALUE

It is great interviewing skills if you can answer a question with examples of achievements in your own work history or in study or even at home or the community. This will show the active side of your personality and demonstrates your value. For example, you might comment on experience installing systems, solving problems, going further by doing something not required, training someone or bringing people together. If you can relate this to creating revenue or saving costs, it becomes very persuasive. But do not just make big claims – you have to be able to go through the steps you took to reach the goal.

HAVE A LIST OF STRENGTHS

Develop a list of your main strengths – this could be anywhere between four or five. You will need detail and examples to back each one up. For the interviewer, these strengths can be the reason you win the job over the competition. It is good to align these strengths with what you know about the company or organisation, and what they list as requirements and attributes for the job.

VARY YOUR LENGTH OF RESPONSES

It is important to give many responses that are perhaps one or two minutes – this is quite long in a conversation but for an interview it shows preparation and commitment. But you should vary the length of responses – making sure some are only one or two sentences. If every answer is a long answer your interviewers will switch off – so carefully choose where longer answers are needed and make sure the pace is varied.

LISTEN CAREFULLY

Stay attentive and if you are not sure what they are getting at, ask them for more information. Listen respectfully and wait for your chance to reply. It can be good to occasionally nod when others make a point you agree with, but do not overdo this.

BE YOURSELF

It is important to genuinely reflect who you really are – any attempt to act like someone else or change your personality will be immediately obvious and will not reflect well. Best to show you are comfortable with who you are – and striving to reach your potential.

GIVE SOME EVIDENCE

Your interviewers will be on the lookout for boasting or grand claims that cannot be supported, so be sure to have evidence to support whatever you say about yourself.

KEEP CONNECTED

During any job interview it is vital to stay alert, maintaining good eye contact, sitting forwards rather than back and show some energy and enthusiasm. If you are leaning back in your chair and staring off through the window, interviewers will feel you are just not interested or even worse that you are arrogant.

ASK QUESTIONS

A good rule in any communication is to ask questions. Most of us rush in with answers, but you can show more empathy and intelligence by using the occasional well thought out question. Prepare some questions before the interview.

BE POSITIVE

It is never good to criticise former employers or colleagues. This comes across as negative or bitter and will turn interviewers against your case. Even if criticism might be justified, it is not the right thing for an interview so learn to stay on the positive.

DEMONSTRATE A "GOOD FIT"

List the requirements of the job point by point, then match your experience to the appropriate requirements. Learn the list and take it in note form if you forget – it can be OK to look at some notes, but not too often. These points work best when they come out progressively during the interview, naturally and spontaneously — rather than run through them in an obviously rehearsed way. Sometimes a less than total match will be overlooked, especially if you stress your enthusiasm to learn.

SHOW INTEREST

Towards the end of the interview, take an opportunity to clearly state that you are interested in the position and would like to go to the next step. Ask what that next step is.

HOW TO ENGAGE COLLEAGUES

Engaging and motivating others – leadership – can often be very different from what at first we think it is. The mindset of real leadership can involve vision, conviction and planning – combined with humility, listening and compassion for others. This mindset is contagious – people love to follow optimism, integrity and connection. By contrast, when we sit in the box of self-imposed limitations our real leadership cannot be seen and we surround ourselves with colleagues who are just as miserable as we feel. How much better would your life be if you had the courage to jump out of that box?

Kiran Mazumdar-Shaw, Chair and Managing Director, Biocon Ltd, has courage and inspires confidence based on conviction: "If you have a vision, a plan and the conviction, you should follow it and success will come to you." The Hindu spiritual leader Mata Amritanandamayi, lovingly called 'Amma', and known globally as India's "hugging saint mother", urges us to bring humility to the table of leadership: "Huge trees are uprooted and buildings collapse in a cyclone, but no matter how strong a cyclone is, it cannot touch the grass. This is the greatness of humility."

Krishnamurti echoes the importance of really listening to others: "So when you are listening to somebody, completely, attentively, then you are listening not only to the words, but also to the feeling of what is being conveyed, to the whole of it, not part of it."

Apple's Steve Jobs described his own leadership role: "The people who are doing the work are the moving force behind the Macintosh. My job is to create a space for them, to clear out the rest of the organization and keep it at bay." There is greater acceptance that people make the difference, that human capital is the big differentiator. This only works if people are inspired by your leadership – if you create the space for them to succeed.

Across all areas, the impact of global markets and intense competition is being felt, the heat is on at the top as customers and shareholders become more demanding. Increasingly, it is to their people as well as technology that they turn for answers. Leaders have to think big, as South African great, Nelson Mandela, reminds us: "There is no passion to be found playing small – in settling for a life that is less than the one you are capable of living."

Everyone around the modern business leader is demanding "better, faster and cheaper". And as leaders turn to their employees, they find that loyalty has been replaced by a free market where employees perform conditionally (am I acknowledged, what do I know, will I be rewarded, is it worth it) rather than as a matter of course. Every day these employees make the choice to either engage of not engage their talents in serving customers and the organisation. Yet many organizations still regard employees as interchangeable units of cost.

The challenge is to inform and motivate, and many in management are not up to it. For this, we can again find inspiration in modern cricket, this time from India's captain, Mahendra Singh Doni: "If you stay cool and calm, it helps the bowler. He looks up to me when things are not going right, and if he finds me cool and calm, then he gets more confidence. It doesn't help if I go and yell at the players. In international cricket, body language is very important. So I try and keep my emotions under check."

The jury is not out on the question of the power of engagement of employees. Engaged employees do produce. The data shows engagement creates more sales, more market value, higher return on capital. On the other side, it shows reduced absenteeism, fewer accidents, greater customer loyalty and retention. These are all direct drivers of profit and success.

But the Gallup Organisation over at least two decades has found that in the west as many as 69% of employees are "not engaged", that only 16% are engaged. This engaged group drive organizational success. The vast majority is not engaged; they drag performance down. The good news is that most people see their workplace as full of potential; they want to learn and make a worthwhile contribution. They also want recognition for that contribution. Most importantly, people want face-to-face communication so they can better understand their place in the organisation.

Who is going to provide the drive for more and more employees to switch to engaged?

How do you motivate people to make the right decisions for customers and the organisation, and how do you unlock the discretionary effort that the "not engaged" might withhold? Here is a daily checklist that can help your leadership to shine:

1. Try to think outside the square, by taking a different view
2. Observe how successful people react in difficult situations
3. Check your mind – are you thinking clearly
4. Be open and honest at all times
5. Take the opportunity to do a bit extra, helping someone

We know from research in a variety of companies exactly what are the communication needs of employees; things like timely and accurate information, coaching and feedback, real communication, a feeling of being valued, understanding of the business and real human contact. And if you think about how employees move to greater loyalty and engagement, it is typically a shift from the personal ("I") to a sense of team and organisation ("We").

Leaders at all levels are obviously the critical

link, rather than just the one at the top. "Leaders" includes managers, supervisors and team leaders. In the day-to-day of the workplace, they are the ones who win or lose discretionary effort and engagement. Unfortunately, most of these leaders, despite their best efforts, have never been trained in communication and have little understanding of it. We all pay lip service to how "vital" communication is; but really more often than not among business leaders communication is poorly understood and badly executed.

On the employee side, a major problem is the sheer volume of information they receive, meaning that they often do not know what to do with it and what it all means. This is the result of communicating without a strategy. Strategic communication is the reverse of this chaotic approach: it brings focus and understanding. Research has shown that what employees are really looking for is "communication" that helps them do their jobs well. They also mostly say that they prefer to get this kind of information from their managers, supervisors and team leaders. So the challenge is how to unlock the power of this opportunity.

There are six imperatives for those who seek to use communication as part of real leadership.

MAKE THE TIME

To say you don't have time to communicate is to say you don't have time to lead. This communication is more than a few memos, emails and meetings. It is vastly more than "my door is always open". A good leader needs a strategy to shape their communication, and then the ability to see it through. Time, persistence and repetition are essential ingredients of good communication.

RELATE IT TO THEM

Naturally employees want to know how information and news relates to them, yet mostly they get swags of information and no help in differentiating it. Information overload and communication failure are team mates. A discussion of developments within your company or organization should include what these developments mean to your team and to their customers. Your people want to know the "why" of things that happen, because with the "why" they can become engaged.

DON'T WAIT TO COMMUNICATE

A massive business leadership problem is secrecy. We are not comfortable as leaders if we do not have all the answers, so we wait until it is too late. The result is always rumour, gossip and declining engagement. For many, the first step to good leadership is a public acknowledgement that you don't know everything. Being comfortable with not having all the answers provides real integrity to your messages. So tell them what you know, tell them what you don't know and tell them when you should know more.

BE OPEN AND HONEST

People have great inbuilt lie detectors. Nothing switches people off quicker than a lie, but this also extends to gossip and "talking big", a failing of those managers who desperately want to impress and think that "if I am a leader I should know everything and be in everything". Much better instead to communicate in a real, open and human way.

WHAT YOU "SAY" SHOULD MATCH WHAT YOU "DO"

Words without matching action are worse than no words at all. You cannot be a leader if you cannot lead by example. Actions speak louder than words. For example, if you promise to do something by a set time, always deliver. At the least, if you cannot deliver explain what has changed and therefore means you cannot deliver as expected – it is worth going out of your way to get this understood. Failure to live up to your promises is a signal to others that they don't need to either.

So, we find that successful leadership becomes a combination of your mindset and your communication skills. You will need to change your mindset – change the way you see yourself. Then your increasing communication skills will allow others to see this change.

5 STEPS TO STRONG COMMUNICATION FOR C-SUITE EXECUTIVES

So you're now in the C-suite of leaders – well done. You are "Chief" of something or maybe you aspire to be. One key to your success will be your ability to influence and lead – which means your communication skills are now under the spotlight.

How many people gain promotion and fail? Generally, we assume they have been promoted above their capability. But in fact even though they won promotion, they stayed in that box of self-imposed limitations and never had the courage to be in the truly vulnerable position of leading others. In this box the core values become fear, lack of trust, criticism, envy and false pride.

C-suite leaders with strong values such as honesty, generosity and patience are more successful – especially when their personal communication is based on truth, friendship and inspiring others.

Kumar Mangalam Birla is the Chairman of The Aditya Birla Group and a man of significant standing in India – he knows the C-suite very well. Do you know what Mr Birla says about leadership? As a future leader, you should know – "Leadership is all about plugging in to the minds and hearts of people. It is about rallying them around to a compelling and exciting vision of the future. It is about upping the imagination of the organisation. It is about encouraging a spirit of intellectual ferment and constructive dissent so that people are not bound by the status quo, and mavericks are given space and free play."

And Sir Richard Branson put it right there – "Communication is the most important skill any leader can possess."

Every C-suite executive and those aspiring to it can become a vastly improved communicator by taking these 5 steps of essential PR:

GET YOUR MESSAGES RIGHT

Many talk about having the "elevator pitch" constantly at the ready, others speak of developing clear key themes for your message. You need to develop these with an external advisor – because internal messages become corporate jargon and are overlooked. The central point is – know who you are, how you are different and what benefit this brings to others. I like to have between six and ten simple sentences that cover my main areas of activity and main messages. Once you have the pitch or the key messages, then keep repeating them until it hurts, because at that point you might just be getting the message across.

MEET PEOPLE

It might be time to review and change your networking priorities. Evaluate what is available – including looking for honorary board positions in the arts or community. Warren Buffett has been a great networker and he describes it in terms of "planting trees" – that is, "someone is sitting in the shade today because someone else planted a tree". Sitting behind the desk does not lead to promotion or success – making connections does. It is not enough to be good at what you are trained for, you need to add being good at communicating, making connections and leading people if you are to head for the C-suite.

YOU HAVE TO BE SOCIAL

Social media impacts every C-suite executive in one way or another. Evaluate this carefully and build a reasonable social media plan. Using vehicles like Facebook and Linked In can work for you so long as you keep your key themes going – monitor the social media chit chat and post "early and often". An out-of-date social media presence – neglected – is a powerfully negative statement, so accept the constant updating social media requires. One of the really positive things you can do on social media is to "share" anything you have found that had an impact on you. People appreciate it, and also gain some insight into how you think and what you stand for.

YOU CAN BE IN MEDIA

If not already, sometime soon the C-suite executive faces the media. So start preparing now – sharpen the messages, get the training, sit in front of a camera. With phones and tablets, you can practice this at home – but make sure you get your peer group friends to look at your performance and give honest feedback. Doing this makes you a better all-round communicator. All the practice in the glare of the lights actually improves every part of your personal communication. Persistence is the key to media presence.

BE HUMAN

Even though you are at or near the top, remember that everything that impacts your ability to succeed is in some way human. Being thoughtful to others, giving the right gift or message at the right time – these all contribute to your reputation. Success comes through adapting to situations and to others, while remaining true to yourself and your values.

All of the above needs to be done with a positive frame of mind – maintaining enthusiasm and a positive mental attitude are such welcome traits in a world of criticism and negativity – so be as bright as you can be and have confidence in you! If you change the way you see yourself, you will then change how others see you. This is the benefit of taking the leap out of that box of restriction. Gaining promotion and leading people are within your potential, so be enthusiastic, value people, relate to others – you will be noticed.

MONEY, SUCCESS, THE GOOD LIFE AND CHANGE

From the best of India and the best of the west we find – money is great if you have it, use it well, but live within your means. It is great to have money in your pocket, but the moment it enters your head you are in trouble – because enough is never enough. So, beware of money taking control of you.

Your attitude to money and success is one part of you – and will be considered by those who can promote you or put you in true leadership roles.

Indian thinker and guru to millions, including several of India's leading business people, Sadhguru Jaggi Vasudev has the best advice here: "Money is empowerment, but by identifying yourself with it, you are making it an impediment. There is nothing wrong with money. If you leave it in your pocket and do not identify with it, it is useful. Once it gets into your head, it becomes a perversion. If you would make your inner well-being the top priority of your life, you would find that money is easily handled."

Success comes from having a passion for what you do, not for how much money you can make. Virgin's Sir Richard Branson has some timely advice here: "Finding gaps in the market, and creating products that make a real difference to people's lives, can only really be accomplished if you have real passion for what you are doing."

Mr Kumar Mangalam Birla, Chairman of The Aditya Birla Group, one of India's leading conglomerates, gives us inspiration on this point: "People contribute when they relate to an organisation, and they relate when they understand the organisation. And people understand an organisation through its values, by experiencing the culture that the values create and by using the systems and processes that the values define."

Values give us stability and direction in the face of change. We cannot hope to succeed if we do not maintain true values, adapting and keeping abreast of changing situations or new trends in our profession or business. The great "Father of the Nation" of India, Mahatma Gandhi urged us to embrace change and become a force for good when he said: "Be the change you want to see in the world".

The great Greek philosopher, Epictetus, found that one key to mental stability and performance was to feel happy with what we have: "Whoever does not regard what he has as most ample wealth, is unhappy, though he be master of the world."

It is good to combine this more relaxed mind with tolerance, as Swami Vivekananda in 1893 told the International Congress of Religions in Chicago: "I am proud to belong to a nation which has taught the world both toleration and universal acceptance. We believe not only in universal toleration but we accept all religions as true."

Will you choose to be flexible in the face of change, while also sticking strongly to core values? This is a good choice. Or will you be so excited by success that you begin to "break the rules" in small ways, laying the foundation for a life of deception? This is a high risk choice, and one that guarantees that even if successful, you will not enjoy it.

Will you be able to enjoy success, without craving it as much as others? This very relaxed attitude seems in some mysterious way to contribute to actual success. Will you use an understanding of impermanence as an antidote to excessive greed and grasping (I want everything!) and ill will (how come they got promoted?) and thereby remain free to focus on the moment? There are so many choices and it is easy to follow the wrong guidance.

Think deeply, remain true to your values and in a rapidly changing world you will have the adaptation skills needed for success. And don't take everything too seriously (including my advice!). Tibet's spiritual leader, the Nobel Prize winner His Holiness the Dalai Lama has expressed this really well: "From early morning until late into the night, even in our dreams, we experience all kinds of perceptions. We go from being relaxed to being anxious, we sometimes feel anger, sometimes desire, other times joy and compassion. We can be sad, then happy. These are transitory states of mind – they are impermanent, they come and go, from moment to moment. But there must be something deeper that is aware of all this – our true Buddha nature – but this is usually hidden by us as we cling to momentary feelings. So we remove the clinging, like opening a curtain, and see our true self. Open, spacious, calm, aware..." Perhaps this point is well understood by successful people?

India's Bhagavad Gita provides a guide, because it calls for us to drop all of our attachment to wanting certain outcomes from our actions – that is, place your focus on what you are doing now, do it as well as you can and results will come. The Gita says: "Better indeed is knowledge than mechanical practice. Better than knowledge is meditation. But better still is surrender of attachment to results, because there follows immediate peace."

Successful entrepreneurs seem to find this peace – they are not constantly staring into some distant future outcome, but instead focus on what they can do today. Western leaders also tell us to set our goals but then to shift focus to the process – the steps – to getting there. Just like the one hundred metre Olympic athletes who concentrate on each step rather than looking at the finishing line.

But why should we focus on the process instead of getting entangled in the results?

Sadhguru has the answer: "When people involve themselves in what they do, they often get entangled. Anything that you associate with, you tend to get identified with. The moment you get identified with something that is not you, you have invested in a system of hallucination that will look and feel real. Once you have invested in a hallucinatory process, your mind will be one continuous mental disorder, as a hallucinatory process can be kept up only with unceasing activity of the mind, and hence, one ends up turning a miracle into madness. The mind is a fabulous miracle; you could hold the universe in it, but generally it ends up as a source of all human misery and the basis of madness and suffering."

Another realization from this change and impermanence is that this lifetime can be short so there is no time to waste. Decide what is important, stick to your values, be honest and true, make effort in the right direction and you will maximize this wonderful life. Sri Sathya Sai Baba with characteristic good humour put it this way: "You must welcome tests because it gives you confidence and it ensures promotion."

Understanding this, let us not waste this opportunity and this precious human life. And that's it. Be a sport, get involved, taking opportunities. Relax. Just relax. Be nice to each other. Try to help people rather than hurt them. Try to get along with them rather than fall out with them. Live your life with love and compassion for others, and something extraordinary will happen! Gandhi summed it all up so beautifully: "Happiness is when what you think, what you say and what you do are in harmony."

Benjamin Franklin was a leading thinker of his time in America, and he said: "By failing to prepare, you are preparing to fail." Picking up that theme, Tagore urges us to take positive action: "You can't cross the sea merely by standing and staring at the water." Is it time for you to take the plunge and to reach your potential?

Mr Kumar Mangalam Birla, Chairman of The Aditya Birla Group, one of India's leading conglomerates, gives us inspiration: "Well, I think the golden rule I can think of is the fact that you must follow your passion and do something that's close to your heart. And I think that that's very important, well, to be successful and to be happy."

Kiran Mazumdar-Shaw, Chair and Managing Director, Biocon Ltd said: "I believe I have created intellectual wealth from very frugal resources and that is what I am acknowledged for. I do hope I can inspire ordinary people to build enterprises from very little monetary resources but a rich mind to succeed. I am proud of having created a valuable organization and that is the wealth I am proud of Biocon is really about building intellectual wealth and not about creating material wealth. It is the opportunity that the company has provided to hundreds of scientists that matter to me."

Her point has been taken up by South Africa's Nelson Mandela who has a great love of education for changing people: "Education is the most powerful weapon which you can use to change the world."

Mother Teresa was once asked why she did not participate in anti-war demonstrations, and her answer provides some insight into how to see a way through this spider web of complex choices that is our life. She said: "I was once asked why I don't participate in anti-war demonstrations. I said that I will never do that, but as soon as you have a pro-peace rally, I'll be there."

Being positive, being "for" something will guide you through life. That is seeing clearly, and I feel the same about "anti-corruption" movements – important as they might be, it is far better to be in favour of something better. But in the process, Mother Teresa also gives a good reminder about being tolerant of others: "I love all religions, but I am in love with my own."

You can see your real value as the ability to deal with life, to negotiate the spider web without getting tangled and caught up in any one thing. That is the formula for success. Too often we see success just in terms of money and possessions, but Sadhguru challenges us to have a different view: "How much you are worth need not be seen in terms of how much you are paid. How much you are worth should be assessed in terms of what responsibilities are given to you. The privilege is not the money that you receive; the privilege is that you have been allowed to create something." This advice is so simple, but it is not easy. We can do it by cutting our attachments to results and things, letting go of outer signs of inner success. This can be our daily practice now, each moment, whatever we are doing, we can practice in the moment, not clinging. This frees you up to deal with this complex spider web of life.

In this way we can feel good about our work, no matter what work the spider web has put our way. Turning again to the Gita, we find:

"No work stains a man who is pure, who is in harmony, who is master of his life, whose soul is one with the soul of all."

CONCLUSION

Scientific research has just discovered that the silk that spiders use to build their webs, trap their prey and dangle from your ceiling is one of the strongest materials known.

But the most important part of the discovery is what makes the spider web so resilient – it is the unusual combination of strength and stretchiness that equals great resilience. Silk first softens and then strengthens when pulled and these properties actually vary depending on the forces applied as well as on the overall web design.

This work was done by Markus Buehler, an associate professor of civil and environmental engineering (CEE) at MIT, who has previously analysed the complex, hierarchical structure of spider silk and its amazing strength – on a pound-for-pound basis, it's stronger than steel.

Now, Buehler and his colleagues have applied their analysis to the structure of the webs themselves, finding evidence of the key properties that make webs so resilient.

Survival, it seems, is not just about being strong – you have to be flexible at times, adaptable, applying strength and gentleness as life demands it.

It turns out, therefore, that the spider's web is a great metaphor for life.

To some extent, we are all born looking out at the world through an existing spider's web – with each strand of the web blocking our complete vision. This is what I mean by being in the box of self-imposed limitation. Many people stay looking at the world in this incomplete way. It is like being born behind bars or in a cage. On top of this, we are just looking through one spider's web and there are billions of them on the planet. So we stay confined.

There is an alternative – jump out of the box – see more clearly, by expanding your mind and your ability to see beyond restrictions. This opens you to your real potential – the exciting potential that each of us have. Your success and happiness in life will largely be determined by your ability to see clearly, understand properly and communicate with great skill – and you cannot do this very well from behind a web or a cage. Get out of the box, and you can truly engage with others – sadly, this rarely happens because when we are locked into the box of limitations we only seek out others who are locked in too. Our resilience declines as our misery increases.

We might be hard-wired to look at the world through restrictions, but I feel our potential shines through when we can see the world for what it is, and see what place we really should occupy in it. In this way, you know that we all live within the complex spider web of life, but your vision is not restricted by the web.

Much of this learning comes from the west and from India. The great twentieth century western scientist, Albert Einstein, had this to say about India: "We owe a lot to Indians, who taught us how to count, without which no worthwhile scientific discovery could have been made." And the American great, Mark Twain, who gave the world so much in terms of easy-to-understand wisdom, said: "India is the cradle of the human race, the birthplace of human speech, the mother of history, grandmother of legend, and great grandmother of tradition. Our most valuable and most instructive materials in the history of man are treasured up in India only."

Real strength comes from very good values such as honesty, generosity and patience, thinking of others. Real power in personal communication comes from speaking with truth, friendship and vision – inspiring others. To get this personal brand – and real strength – you have to jump out of the box of self-imposed limitation and change the way you see yourself – thereby changing how others see you. This mindset allows your real personal brand and leadership to shine through – you become the leader who jumped out of the box.

Stephen Manallack can be contacted via email at stephen@manallack.com.au

Further information is at:

www.facebook.com/stephen.manallack
www.linkedin.com/stephenmanallack
www.eastwestacademy.com.au

Stephen Manallack is a Director of the EastWest Academy and the author of three books including "Soft Skills for a Flat World" published by Tata McGraw-Hill India in December 2012 – providing insights into the "10 mindsets" of Indian business. He serves on the Judging Panel for the Annual Business Awards of the Indian Executive Club in Melbourne. He is currently preparing online GLOBAL COMMUNICATION SKILLS training programs for India and Asia.

Printed in Australia
AUOC02n0743180516
275995AU00001B/1/P